PR
3072
.P6

Porter, Joseph A.

The drama
acts

DATE			

The Drama of Speech Acts

SHAKESPEARE'S LANCASTRIAN TETRALOGY

The Drama of Speech Acts

SHAKESPEARE'S LANCASTRIAN TETRALOGY

BY JOSEPH A. PORTER

UNIVERSITY OF CALIFORNIA PRESS

BERKELEY · LOS ANGELES · LONDON

University of California Press
Berkeley and Los Angeles, California
University of California Press, Ltd.
London, England
Copyright © 1979 by
The Regents of the University of California
ISBN 0-520-03702-2
Library of Congress Catalog Card Number: 78-57310
Printed in the United States of America

1 2 3 4 5 6 7 8 9

❀ Contents

❋ Introduction

I

This study is concerned with the subject of language and speech in *Richard II, 1* and *2 Henry IV,* and *Henry V,* the four plays comprising what is known as Shakespeare's Lancastrian tetralogy. Considering the subject both thematically and dramaturgically, I shall attempt an integrated description and assessment of conceptions and uses of language in these plays. Several initial caveats, explanations, and apologies are in order.

First, there is the question of the propriety of even talking about a "tetralogy," that is, of considering the group as a large aesthetic unity. The question is legitimate in that four plays covering continuous history might not comprise an aesthetic unity like the one I shall discuss here; and indeed that seems the case with the *Henry VI–Richard III* plays. But if the question is so far legitimate, the proof is in the pudding: the Lancastrian plays are a unified tetralogy if one can discover and feel the nature of the unity. And one discovers whatever unity there may be by assuming, in the first place, that there *is* some. If then one's attempt to discover its nature succeeds, the assumption is justified; if not, the question remains open.

It is conceivable, of course, that one might discover evidence of aesthetic *dis*unity; but this seems a riskier claim than unity. With the Lancastrian tetralogy the strictly aesthetic arguments against unity are unconvincing,[1] whereas those studies hypoth-

[1] These arguments mostly concern apparent disunity in the two parts of *H4.* For a survey of views of the relationship between these two plays, see Harold

I

esizing its existence have demonstrated enough to justify the assumption.[2] This appears to be the legitimate answer to the question, and one would like to be able to say no more about it and get on with the business at hand.

Unfortunately I must say a little more. For, it may be objected, I have simply disregarded the strongest argument against taking the tetralogy as an aesthetic whole, namely, the fact that it is difficult or even impossible to imagine that in writing *R2* Shakespeare envisaged the remainder of the tetralogy as we have it; that, indeed, there is good external evidence for supposing that it was not until after the success of *1H4* that he even considered writing the kind of sequel we have. I can anticipate such objections because they have been raised with worrisome frequency before in commentary on the plays. What is worrisome is that such arguments are in fact not strong at all. They seem so, I suspect, because of the large and sophisticated body of bibliographical and historical evidence and deductions they marshal. The evidence is in itself impressive, but not seriously telling against the assumption. To believe that it is presupposes a view of literary creation which naively ignores the possibility of discovery and progressive ordering on the part of an author.

It may well be that in writing *R2* Shakespeare did not foresee the remainder of the tetralogy. But it may also be—and seems likely—that parts of *R2* were written even before other parts of the same play were foreseen. What the "strong" arguments against taking the tetralogy as a whole disregard is that, whether or not Shakespeare had *H5* in his mind as he wrote *R2*, he certainly had *R2* much in his mind as he wrote *H5*. It is true that initially he would have known that he was beginning a play, *R2*, and might not have known he was beginning a tetralogy, but this simply means that one must posit a different kind of aesthetic unity, one perhaps resulting to a greater extent from exploration and discovery, progressive and retrospective ordering,

---

Jenkins, *The Structural Problem in Shakespeare's Henry the Fourth*, pp. 2–5. Full references to this and other works cited can be found in the Selective Bibliography.

[2]See, for example, Joan Webber, "The Renewal of the King's Symbolic Role," and James Winney, *The Player King*.

for a tetralogy comprising relatively self-sufficient plays than for a play comprising scenes which are not at all self-sufficient.

In the four chapters on the individual plays that follow I try as far as possible to maintain the sort of double vision needed to do justice both to the integrity of the tetralogy and to that of each play, using a certain amount of systematic ambiguity or alternation of focus between play and tetralogy. There is also a degree of flexibility in distribution of attention within the chapters on the individual plays which would be inappropriate were the large design of the tetralogy not also in view. For instance, in the chapter on 1H4 Falstaff is somewhat slighted; but the slight is at least partly remedied by the attention given him in the chapter on 2H4. On the other hand, the different formats of these chapters are intended to reflect the self-sufficiency of the four plays, as well as the changing requirements of the reader of this study (e.g., the chapter on R2 is long because there the reader is introduced to my methods).

Since building up an integrated description of ways of conceiving of and using language in the tetralogy will involve attention to a large number of details and considerable close analysis of portions of the text, and thus the unity might not always be apparent, I shall make use of a frame of reference consisting of three "summary metaphors" or analogues for the action.

The first of these derives from Tillyard's view that the tetralogy represents or enacts the historical movement from the Middle Ages to the Renaissance.[3] Tillyard uses this metaphor as a convenient handle for summarizing the changing conceptions of kingship and social order in the tetralogy; here I shall use it more to summarize changes in ways of conceiving of and using language—changes analogous to the demise of the universal authoritative language of Latin and the concurrent rise of the vernaculars.

The second analogue is closely parallel to this. It is the story of the building of the Tower of Babel and its fall with the proliferation of tongues. Of the three analogues, the Babel story will be invoked most often, for, while neatly encapsulating much of the

[3]E. M. W. Tillyard, *Shakespeare's History Plays.*

same material as the medieval-Renaissance analogue, it also adds a moral dimension, with its suggestion that the proliferation of tongues is a retribution for presumption.[4]

This element of morality is also present in the third analogue, that of the Fall, whose story summarizes certain ways in which Richard's linguistic situation is analogous to that of Adam in Eden, with his privileges of talking with God and of assigning names to the parts of creation. It also summarizes ways in which the Henrys' linguistic procedure is more time-conscious and less absolutist than Richard's.

The discussion of the tetralogy in chapters 1 to 4 does not depend on the assumption that these analogues were present in Shakespeare's mind or that they should be in ours as we regard the plays. However, in Chapter 5 I consider the question of whether more ought to be made of them, especially the two Biblical stories. The Fall is directly alluded to on a number of occasions in the tetralogy; and, while Shakespeare never, I believe, alludes directly to the Babel story, there are several passages suggesting that he had this story in the back of his mind as he wrote these plays. Nevertheless, at least until Chapter 5, these three analogues can be taken as mere expository conveniences.

[4]The Babel story:

> Then the whole earth was of one language and one speech. And as they went from the East, they found a plaine in the land of Shinar, and there they abode. And they said one to another, Come, let us make bricke and burne it in the fire, so they had bricke for stone, and slime had they in stead of morter. Also they said, Goe to, let us builde us a citie and a tower, whose top may reach unto the heaven, that wee may get us a name, least wee be scattered upon the whole earth. But the Lord came downe, to see the citie and tower which the sonnes of men builded. And the Lord said, Behold, the people is one, and they all have one language, and this they begin to doe, neither can they be stopped from whatsoever they have imagined to do. Come on, let us goe downe, and there confound their language, that every one perceive not anothers speach. So the Lord scattered them from thence upon all the earth, and they left off to build the citie. Therefore the name of it was called Babel, because the Lord did there confound the language of all the earth: from thence did the Lord scatter them upon all the earth.
>
> (Gen. 11:1–9; from the 1599 Genevan Bible in Alderman Library, University of Virginia, Charlottesville.)

I shall also, in chapters 1 to 4, be using a conceptual machinery derived from recent developments in British and American linguistic philosophy, of which the central notion is that of "speech act" taken from the work of J. L. Austin.[5] This conceptual machinery is in no sense an expository convenience like the "summary metaphors," but rather is essential in the methodology. In using this conceptual framework I try to keep the study as free of unfamiliar terminology as possible, but when much of the argument is fairly technical analysis, a certain amount of technical terminology is unavoidable. Therefore in the second half of this introduction I expound Austin's idea of the "speech act." This provides a basic conceptual apparatus to which I make additions as needed in the body of the work.

In Chapter 5, after the reader has seen this conceptual framework used extensively and in detail, I try to place my approach in relation to certain more familiar kinds of approaches current in Shakespeare criticism. Finally, in Chapter 6, I return for a last look at the tetralogy, summarizing and tying up loose ends as I consider the overall design of the work "metadramatically," that is, as manifesting an argument about language with respect to the genre of drama.

Textual citations throughout for the Lancastrian plays are from the New Arden editions,[6] a choice that reflects the audience to whom this study is directed—not exclusively specialists (who, in any case, should find these texts manageable and much of the supplementary material useful), but also other serious readers of Shakespeare for whom, at present, these are the most helpful editions available.

[5]Primarily from *How to Do Things with Words*, but also from *Philosophical Papers*.

[6]*King Richard II*, ed. Peter Ure; *The First Part of King Henry IV*, ed. A. R. Humphreys; *The Second Part of King Henry IV*, ed. Humphreys; *King Henry V*, ed. J. H. Walter. For the other plays mentioned, I have used *William Shakespeare: The Complete Works*, ed. Charles Jasper Sisson. Regarding the supplementary material—introductions, notes, appendices—on the basis of which the editions of the tetralogy were chosen for textual citation, Walter seems the most solidly helpful. Ure sometimes interprets and glosses with an assurance perhaps better suited to a critical study than an edition. Humphreys sometimes arbitrarily burdens his notes with information of questionable relevance.

II

. . . 'tis a kind of good deed to say well,
And yet words are no deeds.
   Henry to Wolsey in Shakespeare's Henry VIII

. . . this artistic miracle can only occur if the playwright
finds words that are spoken action.
   Luigi Pirandello[7]

The present study depends heavily on the concept of the "speech act" which comes from the work of the British philosopher J. L. Austin, "the most influential (from a methodological point of view) of ordinary-language philosophers."[8] Austin's work has been so influential that "speech act" is recognized by philosophers as a semitechnical term; but even to them, it is only semitechnical, and its import remains partly discretionary.

A speech act is an act performed in speech. The concept was isolated and discussed intensively by Austin in *How to Do Things with Words* (1962). He begins by analyzing utterances of the form "I hereby christen (deny, accuse, etc.) . . . ," calling these utterances "performatives." They interest him because they cannot be accounted for by a traditional—and to Austin, simplistic— view of language, a view according to which either an utterance is true or false (i.e., "descriptive"), or it falls into a category of "emotive-expressive-nonsensical" utterances such as "Ouch!" or "That's a splendid Van Gogh." An utterance like "I hereby christen this ship the *Queen Mary*" may go right or wrong in various ways, but it is properly neither true nor false (no one could object "That's not true") nor yet "emotive-expressive-nonsensical."

Austin notices two further things about performatives. First, they are *acts*—christening, denial, accusation, and the like— done in speech. (This is related to their lack of truth or falsity: an act may be successful, proper, etc., but not true.) Second, in a performative the act is done *explicitly:* we make the act of chris-

---

[7]From an article "Spoken Action" ("Azione parlata") written in 1899, translated by Fabrizio Melano for *The Theory of the Modern Stage*, ed. Eric Bentley (Harmondsworth, Eng., 1968).
[8]Richard Rorty, "Preface," *The Linguistic Turn;* see n. 5.

tening explicit when we do it with the word "christen." However, as Austin points out, the acts which are done explicitly in performatives may also be done nonexplicitly. Christening, for instance, might be done with the sentence "This ship is now the *Queen Mary.*" What is constant, whether or not it is made explicit, is the *force* of the utterance, or the *kind of act* it does— christening, in the examples here. Austin calls such acts "speech acts." He also calls them "illocutionary acts," since they are performed *in* speech.

It is important to note that in performing an illocutionary act a person also performs the act of uttering a sentence, the simple act of speech itself. Austin terms this the "locutionary act." Thus the illocutionary act of (explicitly) urging may involve the locutionary act of uttering the sentence "I urge you to X." Furthermore, in performing both these acts one may be performing a third, namely, the act of persuasion. Persuasion is an example of what Austin calls a "perlocutionary act," one done *through* speech. (That it is not done *in* an utterance, as is, say, denial, is suggested by the impossibility of finding an explicit act of persuasion; that is, we cannot say "I hereby persuade you to X.") Anything like a systematic description of this third sort of act— involving not only the speaker but also typically the reaction of the hearer—seems impossible, at least at present.

"Speech act," then, as Austin usually means it, and as I shall mean it, is of the illocutionary act type in Austin's paradigm:

> . . . Locution
> He said to me "Shoot her!" . . .
> . . . Illocution
> He urged (or advised, ordered, &c.) me to shoot her.
> . . . Perlocution
> He persuaded me to shoot her.[9]

Austin's work thus provides a way of considering the action done in speech, and does so systematically insofar as (1) in almost every utterance, as he suggests, some speech act is done, and speech acts are done only in speech; and (2) since it is done only in language, speech action (unlike nonverbal action) is patterned in basically linguistic ways—for instance, a speech act, as

[9]*How to Do Things with Words*, p. 101.

we have seen, is either explicit or inexplicit, depending on whether or not it is performed with a word that names it. Or, to put the matter another way, Austin's work defines a realm— speech action—in which verbal drama takes shape, and describes some of that realm's primitive elements—features such as explicitness-inexplicitness. Or, to put it a third way, Austin's work is of potential value to us here because he is dealing with *dramatic* facts about language (even using examples from Shakespeare). In this respect his work contrasts with several other recent additions to our understanding of language, some within literary criticism, such as studies of iterative imagery, and some without, such as the theory of transformational generative grammar.[10]

However, some obstacles to fulfilling the promise of Austin's work are immediately apparent. First is the incompleteness of Austin's own discussion of speech acts: he seems to raise more questions than he answers. The central, basic part of his theory is set forth clearly and with certainty, but concerning other parts Austin himself had doubts. We do not have a fully articulated and developed theory-machine ready to put to work.

Philosophers have, of course, discussed Austin's work and in some cases developed it further[11]; nevertheless, pursuing commentary on his work in philosophical journals has not proved useful. Even in Austin himself there are certain aspects of the theory which, though of considerable importance within linguistic philosophy, are not of great concern to the literary critic. And the commentary on his work seems (perhaps inevitably) to criticize, assess, and elaborate the theory in ways that lessen its usefulness for us. This is to an extent the case even with John R. Searle's *Speech Acts: An Essay in the Philosophy of Language* (1969) which, since it is the fullest and most elaborate development and critique of Austin's theory, I have taken into consideration and at one point (Chapter 4) used in some detail. Nor, in any

[10]That conceptual machinery is used occasionally (sparingly) in the present study.

[11]Rorty, with four articles on Austin and an introduction in which he is discussed at some length, presents a good introductory picture of what other philosophers have made of Austin's work. John R. Searle, especially in *Speech Acts*, seems to have developed Austin's theories most fruitfully.

case, is Austin's theory yet "complete" in any generally accepted sense.

Yet all this is to say that Austin's theory, his body of related insights, is well suited for our purposes, because it has a breadth of applicability of which we may take advantage. Furthermore, because Austin's theory is in a sense unfinished we can the more easily have a good conscience about developing it to meet our needs, as I now attempt to do.[12]

We need not concern ourselves, as Austin does, with contrasting illocutionary force with truth-value; for that contrast, of however great relevance to the philosophy of language, is not especially relevant in the criticism of drama. We want a dramatic rather than a philosophical theory, and to achieve this it will be helpful to define speech action further than Austin does, using the following contrast. While acts such as christening and denial are done *in* language, there are also others done as it were *on* language—acts such as punning, rhyming, and the like. The former seem in conception to involve essential reference to the speaker-hearer axis; this is clearly true of acts like urging and welcoming, and a case could also be made for an act like christening. By contrast an act like punning seems conceptually to involve essential reference to the speaker-utterance axis. Now, while punning could presumably be included under the rubric "speech act," I shall not do so, because there seems to be nothing essentially dramatic about the speaker-utterance relation. The speaker-hearer axis, on the other hand, does seem essentially dramatic, and therefore my rule of thumb will be to keep that relation in view and to consider only those "speech acts" which in conception involve essential reference to it.

A second criterion which makes roughly the same distinction is the ability of the verb naming the act—when there is such a verb—to take a personal (direct or indirect) object. Thus the speech acts with which I am concerned can be referred to in

---

[12]Since the present study was begun, a number of other writers have addressed themselves to questions of the usefulness of speech-act theory in literary criticism. For a good overview (with a speech-act analysis of *Coriolanus*), see Stanley E. Fish, "How to Do Things with Austin and Searle." The first book-length essay in speech-act criticism (I have not seen it) is Mary Louise Pratt, *Toward a Speech Act Theory of Literary Discourse*.

sentences like "He warns you," "He told you." The "speech acts" I exclude are without such objects: those ordinarily referred to in sentences like "He puns," "He ranted."

Matters can be clarified further. Given the idea of speech acts, what interests us is their dramatic parameters—the dimensions in which they exist. I have already mentioned one such parameter, *kind of illocutionary force*. Austin, in the final sections of *How to Do Things with Words*, divides speech acts into five provisional categories according to illocutionary force, so that this parameter is five-valued.[13] The problem here, however, is that the taxonomy is only a sketch and, even more, that the five kinds tend to shade into one another, making the parameter indeterminately many-valued rather than five-valued; all this uncertainty and indistinctness lessens the value of the parameter.

A different parameter expounded by Austin is that of *explicitness*. And this parameter is clearly two-valued: a speech act is either explicit or inexplicit and there seem to be no borderline cases. Another parameter, one of great importance in dealing with the drama and yet practically ignored by Austin, is *direction of address*. If we think of the speaker, the act can be directed to anyone on stage or, with apostrophe, to anyone or anything, so that this parameter might seem to be indeterminately many-valued. However, from the standpoint of a hearer, the parameter can be distinctly two-valued: either an act is directed toward him or it is not.

In general, then, for the sake of simplicity and clarity, I shall be considering two-valued parameters of speech action; others will be used more cautiously.

Such, and so modified, is J. L. Austin's theory on which I depend more or less continually (even through long stretches where I do not allude to it) in the pages that follow. And, more than might be apparent, I look also to Austin's writing for the example of its spirit and style—unassuming, stubborn, and friendly.

[13]For later taxonomies of illocutionary force, see Searle, "A Taxonomy of Illocutionary Acts"; Richard Ohmann, "Instrumental Style"; and B. G. Campbell, "Toward a Workable Taxonomy of Illocutionary Forces."

CHAPTER ONE

✵ *Richard II*

Much more than the rest of the tetralogy, *Richard II* has struck commentators with the important role played in it by the subject of language, and attention in this direction has increased steadily, especially in recent decades.[1] Changing contexts warrant different justifications for pursuing an investigation: whereas earlier the subject of language in *R2* might have seemed questionably narrow and separate from the "major issues" of the play, by now, with the increasing awareness that language is in fact a "major issue," one needs to defend the traversing of ground that may already seem well-trodden. My justification is the belief that the uncharted portion of the territory is large enough to admit much further exploration, including that undertaken here.

Richard's situation represents a starting point not only politically but also linguistically for the entire tetralogy—a thesis for the dialectic of the remaining plays. Therefore I shall be most concerned here to get at the nature of this thesis, which is by no means simple.[2] Most of this chapter, then, consists of analysis of

[1]See, for example, Richard Altick, "Symphonic Imagery in *R2*"; Wolfgang Clemen, *The Development of Shakespeare's Imagery*; Ernst H. Kantorowicz, *The King's Two Bodies*; Eric La Guardia, "Ceremony and History"; Molly Maureen Mahood, *Shakespeare's Wordplay*; Derek A. Traversi, *Shakespeare from Richard II to Henry V*; and James Winny, *The Player King*. More recently, this direction of attention appears in "*Richard II*: The Fall of Speech," the last chapter of James L. Calderwood's remarkably suggestive *Shakespearean Metadrama*.

[2]Calderwood, for example, calls it a "metadramatic" handling of problems of

Richard's speech alone. Even without regard to the remainder of
the tetralogy, such an emphasis would be justified by the king's
predominance in the play. Still, *R2* is not a "monodrama," and I
shall naturally consider the other characters and the action in
general in the course of dealing with Richard.

I

Talk of name, naming, title, and the like constitutes
easily the most prominent body of references to language in the
play.[3] Indeed the topic arises so frequently in the dialogue that
one can trace the general course of the action in terms of it, and
so provide a basis for further investigation, as follows.

Bolingbroke—the future Henry IV—and Mowbray come before Richard "to appeal each other of high treason" (I.i.27).[4]
Bolingbroke is perhaps the initiator of the action, since his "appeal" is mentioned first (ll. 4, 9). This word introduces the topic
of name: as a noun it means something like "accusation," but
with Bolingbroke's "Come I appellant" (l. 34) we see that at least
in this world accusation is essentially name giving. Bolingbroke
makes this still clearer as he goes on to say

> Thou art a traitor and a miscreant,
> · · · · · · · · · ·
> Once more, the more to aggravate the note,
> With a foul traitor's name stuff I thy throat.
> (I.i.39–44)

Gages are exchanged. The proof of the appellation is to come in
a tournament; the "happiness," to use Austin's term,[5] of the

the degradation of poetry by the genre of drama and, as such, the culmination of
a dialectic traced through *Titus Andronicus, Love's Labour's Lost, Romeo and Juliet,*
and *A Midsummer Night's Dream*

[3]And the one most discussed in the criticism: see especially Winny and
Calderwood.

[4]Textual citations throughout, unless otherwise noted, are from the New
Arden editions (see Introduction, n. 6, and Selective Bibliography).

[5]For Austin, a speech act is "happy" or "felicitous" if it goes right, is not, for
example, vitiated by attendant circumstances:

> A good many . . . things have as a general rule to be right and to go
> right if we are to be said to have happily brought off our action. What
> these are we may hope to discover by looking at and classifying types

respective namings is to depend on the outcome of the fight. God is to determine the giver of the right name by making him victorious; the name "traitor" is to apply to one of the combatants at his death. Although the name has been uttered, it does not yet apply—is not yet recognized by the society as applying. It seems to hover in the air waiting to alight and stick. Further, there is a peculiar reflexivity about the name, since to call someone a traitor falsely is to be a traitor oneself. Richard suggests that one of them must be guilty:

> We thank you both, yet one but flatters us,
> As well appeareth by the cause you come,
> Namely, to appeal each other of high treason.
>   (I.i.25–27)

His remark is interesting incidentally because of his "namely" and more importantly because it shows that to him the misdeed is not treason but flattery—the first of many characteristic oddities of thought which we shall note in him.

Such, roughly, is the opening action. Perhaps it is better termed a "situation," since the accusations had been made before the time of the opening scene; but they become official as we hear them delivered in the king's presence. In any case, Richard's first clear "action"—one difficult to fathom—is an attempt to reconcile the opponents. This is to say that he attempts to halt the name's "taking hold" even when he assumes that one of the opponents "but flatters" him. "Wrath-kindled gentlemen, be rul'd by me" (l. 152) he says, and "let this end where it begun" (l. 158). He and Gaunt tell the opponents to throw down one another's gages, but neither obeys, not even when Richard commands a second time, "throw down we bid, there is no boot" (l. 164).

---

of case in which something *goes wrong* and the act—marrying, betting, bequeathing, christening, or what not—is therefore at least to some extent a failure: the utterance is then, we may say, not indeed false but in general *unhappy*. And for this reason we call the doctrine of *the things that can be and go wrong* on the occasion of such utterances, the doctrine of the *Infelicities*.

(*How to Do Things with Words*, p. 14)

For elaborations of Austin's theory of the happiness of speech acts, see the following writings by John Searle: *Speech Acts*, "A Taxonomy of Illocutionary Acts," and "Indirect Speech Acts."

Both men claim that they are unable to obey. Richard has in a sense asked them to do the impossible, to reverse or ignore time. Once the name is out in the open, something must be done with it. Unless it is made to apply, the situation is intolerable. Nor can the name be taken back by either appellant, for to do so is virtually to accept it oneself. Mowbray's

> Myself I throw, dread sovereign, at thy foot;
> My life thou shalt command, but not my shame.
> The one my duty owes, but my fair name,
> Despite of death . . .
> To dark dishonour's use thou shalt not have
>   (I.i.165–69)

puts these aspects of the matter eloquently.

Much of the reciprocal accusation in this scene concerns the death of the Duke of Gloucester, Richard's and Bolingbroke's uncle and the former's severest critic. Though Gloucester's death at Calais while Mowbray was there in command seems to have been an execution ordered by Richard, the king never admits any responsibility for it, so that the event remains somewhat ambiguous throughout the play. It may be that Richard seeks to maintain this ambiguity in attempting to reconcile Bolingbroke and Mowbray, since the shame of the title "traitor," whether it applies to his lieutenant or to his cousin, redounds to an extent on Richard himself. In any case, both Bolingbroke and Mowbray are more willing than Richard to trust in the will of God, and in spite of the king's "bid" they will not be reconciled. Thus the opening scene ends with Richard's lamely commanding that which apparently cannot be otherwise:

> Be ready, as your lives shall answer it,
> At Coventry upon Saint Lambert's day.
> · · · · · · · · · · ·
> Since we cannot atone you, we shall see
> Justice design the victor's chivalry.
>   (I.i.198–203)

There follows a short scene of dialogue between Gloucester's widow and John of Gaunt. Gaunt appears certain that Richard is responsible for Gloucester's death, but he, like his son, urges,

"Put we our quarrel to the will of heaven" (I.ii.6). In her reply the widow touches repeatedly on the idea of naming:

> Call it not patience, Gaunt, it is despair . . .
> . . . .
> That which in mean men we intitle patience
> Is pale cold cowardice in noble breasts.
> (I.ii.29–34)

It is as though the principle of the applicability of names has been generally unbalanced in the realm. The name "traitor" floats in the air and it seems that Richard is ultimately at fault; yet the name cannot apply to him for treason is *against* the king. Theories of reference totter in the face of such a paradox.

Nevertheless, there is the possibility that the will of God will manifest itself in the tournament. The next scene begins with the ceremonious presentation of the combatants, in which their names are prominent: "What is thy name? and wherefore com'st thou hither" (I.iii.31). All seems about to be resolved until Richard halts the ceremony in its midst. This time he succeeds in thwarting the wills of the combatants and, apparently, that of God, as he banishes Mowbray and Bolingbroke. He instructs them to swear

> . . . the oath that we administer:
> You never shall, so help you truth and God,
> Embrace each other's love in banishment
> (I.iii.182–84)

in perfect contradiction to his earlier command that they be friends. Through Richard's self-contradiction we can see his main object: that the tournament should not take place, that the name "traitor" should not stick. If he cannot transform incipient civil strife into concord, then he will not allow it to be civil: it must not be admitted, much less resolved, in his realm. But he is perfectly willing that there be discord outside his realm—indeed he demands it.

His procedure here is characteristic of him. There are already suggestions of something like an equivalence between the realm of England and Richard's consciousness or the scope of his attention. He thrusts difficulty or potential difficulty alike from his presence, his realm and his consciousness. It is then entirely consistent, supposing Richard ultimately responsible for Gloucester's death, that the crime should have been committed outside England, and that he never even shows an awareness that it has occurred.[6]

After the sentence of banishment Bolingbroke and Gaunt take leave of one another and the idea of naming arises again. Their exchange is much like the earlier one between Gaunt and Gloucester's widow, with Gaunt advocating a kind of Stoic patience. Here, even more explicitly than before, this patience amounts to nomenclature:

> *Gaunt.* Call it a travel that thou tak'st for pleasure.
> (I.iii.263)

But Bolingbroke like the duchess is unable to accept such advice:

> *Bolingbroke.* My heart will sigh when I miscall it so,
>   Which finds it an inforced pilgrimage.
> (I.iii.264–65)

What Gaunt has urged of his son and the duchess is that they assume the privilege of assigning names (or "calling"), a privilege like that of Adam in Eden, and one that Richard himself has to some extent arrogated. But the son's and the widow's refusals imply that in a social and fallen world this privilege may be barren.

Thus Gaunt, Richard's best spokesman, is unable to promulgate the reigning conception of language. Accusations have to do with real events; they are provable and remain at issue regardless of Richard's attempt to dissolve them: one cannot long "cloy the hungry edge of appetite / By bare imagination of a feast." Names and serious accusations are too deeply involved with nonverbal reality to be completely subject to the individual's whim. The best Gaunt can do then is to turn back to Richard with prophetic warning; and his own end gives a foretaste of Richard's: "sick men play with their names."

Ideas of name and naming thus figure very prominently in

---

[6]And this is noteworthy because the question of guilt is raised, and because elsewhere almost without exception it is Shakespeare's practice to have evildoers admit, show consciousness of, their misdeeds—in soliloquy or otherwise.

the first large movement of the plot. Richard himself has not yet said much on the subject, though he provokes most of the discussion and is deeply involved in the process of nomenclature in the realm. But in the remainder of the play, as his difficulties increase, he comes to speak more often of names, especially his own. These moments mark the stages of his tragedy: his displeasure at first hearing criticism from Gaunt—

> Can sick men play so nicely with their names?
>   (II.i.84)

his faltering assurance—

> I had forgot myself, am I not king?
> Awake, thou coward majesty! thou sleepest.
> Is not the king's name twenty thousand names?
> Arm, arm, my name! a puny subject strikes
> At thy great glory;
>   (III.ii.83–86)

his increased despair—

>   O that I were as great
> As is my grief, or lesser than my name!
>   (III.iii.136–37)

> What must the king do now? Must he submit?
> The king shall do it. Must he be depos'd?
> The king shall be contented. Must he lose
> The name of king? a god's name, let it go;
>   (III.iii.143–46)

his abdication—

>   I have no name, no title;
> No, not that name was given me at the font,
> But 'tis usurp'd. Alack the heavy day,
> That I have worn so many winters out,
> And know not now what name to call myself!
>   (IV.i.255–59)

Furthermore, at crucial points in the later action of the other major characters name and name change is emphasized. At Gaunt's death Richard seizes his property, which Bolingbroke should have inherited, and, apparently because of the appropriation, Bolingbroke returns from exile. He talks, however, less about the property than about something else he inherits from his father—the title Duke of Lancaster. He will not so much as answer to his old title of "Herford":

> *Berkeley.* My Lord of Herford, my message is to you.
> *Bolingbroke.* My lord, my answer is—to Lancaster,
> And I am come to seek that name in England,
> And I must find that title in your tongue,
> Before I make reply to aught you say.
> (II.iii.69–73)

What may here seem perverse fastidiousness in Bolingbroke begins to look more like legalistic shrewdness when we see him replying to York's condemnation of his return with

> As I was banish'd, I was banish'd Herford
> But as I come, I come for Lancaster.
> (II.iii.112–13)

Bolingbroke would have his title totally identify him, have Richard's sentence apply to the-holder-of-the-title-"Herford" and not to the-holder-of-the-title-"Lancaster." Given his odd premise he is perfectly justified—we might think him guilty of hedging had Richard called him by his unalterable surname "Bolingbroke," but heretofore Richard has referred to him only as "Herford." Nor does Richard attempt to beat him at this game by calling him "Herford" now; to Richard he is henceforth only "Bolingbroke" and "King Henry."

Thus to the three characters who loom largest in the play—Richard, Gaunt, and Bolingbroke—the idea of name is of great importance. There are numerous similarities and contrasts between them to be drawn. Consider Ernst H. Kantorowicz's suggestion that there is "a curious change in Richard's attitude—as it were, a metamorphosis from 'Realism' to 'Nominalism.'"[7] The idea is useful and, turning to Gaunt and Bolingbroke, I would say that the former seems a nominalist and the latter a realist. In particular there are striking similarities between Gaunt and the later Richard. The king who, for instance, was disturbed to see Gaunt playing with his own name, comes in time to the more radical game of playing with the

[7]*The King's Two Bodies,* Chap. 2.

pronoun "I" (see below, p. 25). Yet throughout, Richard seems to share with Bolingbroke the insistence on a one-to-one relationship between name and thing. Alternatively, Richard throughout is much like Gaunt in the insistence on his own ability to assign names. To an extent, then, he comprehends a polarity whose extremes we can see embodied in Bolingbroke and Gaunt.

As even this brief survey shows, the topic of name in *R2* might be called a controlling idea or theme of the play. The plot or "story" is, in the large, *about* name inasmuch as name is crucially at issue in many of the large events, situations, and turning points of the action. Much of the local and subsidiary action in which the "story" is embodied is similarly about name. Repeatedly, even at junctures where the story is not obviously about this topic, stages in the course of the action are marked by its appearance in the dialogue.

The investigation of the topic could be carried much farther. Since, however, the mere spatial delineation of such themes is a familiar procedure, and since, as we shall see, "name" is but one facet of a much larger unifying theme, we may have reached a point of diminishing returns. Therefore, we may now probe a little deeper by considering the relevance of this central topic to the central character.

II

In the first place, what *is* the name Richard speaks most about? Primarily it is the name "King." With this name as with "Mother," "Father," "God," we have a peculiar situation in which there is no need for a distinction between common and proper noun since (normally) for any speaker there is but one representative of the class named by the common noun. Richard plays obsessively with apparent contradictions of this fact in the name "King."[8]

[8]Especially in the deposition scene as with

> God save the king! although I be not he;
> And yet, amen, if heaven do think him me,
>   (IV.i.174–75)

and also at IV.i.162, 220, 305–8.

There is also the name "Richard," and it is doubtless this to which Richard refers when he says

> I have no name, no title;
> No, not that name was given me at the font.
> (IV.i.255–56)

One's proper name is something one has, something which one was given. That one must depend upon others for his own name is one of the most important facts of name dealt with in *R2*. It would seem that this dependence is virtually intolerable to Richard himself.

It may be that in calling "King" a name we are confusing name and title—"Captain," say, seems clearly a title, and "Joseph" a name. But the distinction is not always so clear or applicable, especially in cases like "Father" and "King." "King" seems much more like "Father" than like "Captain," considering the almost universal metaphor of king as father of his country. In any case, the confusion, if there is one, pervades the play.

The distinction we ordinarily recognize between the name and title of a person has, of course, something to do with the occasion and manner of bestowal. There are in fact great differences in the ways one depends on others for his "name." The name "Richard," bestowed at the font, cannot be taken away by the bestower. The name "King," given in a sense by God and the realm at coronation, can perhaps be taken away, at least by the community. We have already seen some of the complexities involved in the bestowal of such names as "traitor."

Richard, however, tends to disregard the variety of the ways in which one is given names. In his mind various types of nomenclature tend to coalesce so that to give up the name "King" is also to give up the name "Richard" bestowed at the font. This is absurd—a conceit—since he cannot relinquish "Richard" as he does "King." But conceits are revealing, and the precise way in which Richard flies in the face of fact here is characteristic of much of his thought. His fanciful demand for identity between his names, regardless of attendant circumstances, is but one instance of a way of conceiving of language that in certain respects is monstrously simplistic.

Like surnames, the name "King" is normally inherited; it is in this respect that both surnames and titles like "King" are perhaps most like property. As we have seen, Bolingbroke is very much conscious of this feature of names; in his mind the name and the property go together. But Richard, in annexing Gaunt's property at least, seems to ignore the importance of inheritance. In this connection it is interesting to note that, for all his claims to be the rightful king, Richard does not base his claim on inheritance.[9]

Although one can be said to "have" a name, it was not only bestowed by others but in a sense is also used primarily by others—it can be seen as a convenience to the community, a convention. In another sense one's name is a kind of extension of the self. The king affects the realm by orders sent down through the hierarchies, orders which the king's name identifies as having to be obeyed as they pass in reports from mouth to mouth: "The king wishes . . . ," "The king has decreed . . . ," and so on. Even in informal reports, the king's name serves as a marker of legitimacy, identifying that which is to be accepted and passed on, like the special markings on currency. Richard is aware of these matters, and he likens his word to coin of the realm: "And if my word be sterling yet in England" (IV.i.264). He regards his name as an extension of himself, but it is intolerable to him that the name should be used, as well as given, by others. And, generally, when he thinks of his dealings with the community he seems to concentrate on the importance of his name, to the perilous exclusion of all else.

Personal pronouns constitute "names" of another sort; and Richard's pronouns are interesting throughout. The first person overwhelmingly dominates his speech, as we might expect. Early in the play he usually employs the royal plural. It is probable that the form normally marks some genuine intended plural that includes others with the speaker—something like "I and my realm"—and is related to such customs as calling the king of England simply "England."[10] The royal "we" would then be

[9]Indeed he never refers to his father, as if, like Christ to whom he insistently compares himself, he has none on earth.

[10]For an interesting brief account of the European history of the royal plural, and some suggestions of its conceptual relation to other first person plurals, see Otto Jespersen, *The Philosophy of Grammar*, pp. 192–93.

explicable in terms of the general grammar of the language. However, while some of Richard's "we"'s *could* be read as "ego+other," he on occasion uses "we" so as to make this meaning impossible.

There are suggestions of such a usage in the "our blood" and "our presence" of the first act, although blood and presence can reasonably be considered communal. It is in the first scene of the second act, at a peculiarly charged moment, that Richard for the first time indisputably uses "we" as a surface marker for "ego." Gaunt lies on his deathbed and, believing that

> the tongues of dying men
> Inforce attention like deep harmony,
>   (II.i.5–6)

he delivers to Richard the first criticism and accusation the king has heard. He says that Richard too is dying:

> Thy death-bed is no lesser than thy land,
> Wherein thou liest in reputation sick.
>   (II.i.95–96)

Richard listens as the tirade mounts to name giving—

> Landlord of England art thou now, not king,
> Thy state of law is bondslave to the law,
> And thou—
>   (II.i.113–15)

whereupon he interrupts with

> A lunatic lean-witted fool,
> Presuming on an ague's privilege,
> Darest with thy frozen admonition
> Make pale our cheek, chasing the royal blood
> With fury from his native residence.
>   (II.i.115–19)

Gaunt's repeated "thou" (he alone addresses the king so) draws our attention to personal pronouns, by which we are well repaid. Beyond Richard's odd deformation of Gaunt's "thou"— "as if it referred to Gaunt himself"[11]—there is the fact that nothing can be communal about Richard's "our." Something

---

[11]Peter Ure's note on the passage in the New Arden edition.

strange has happened here. The surface form can no longer have its normal function. Thus in Richard's language there is no single surface marker to realize distinctively the semantic combination "ego+other." We may then wonder whether Richard's "we" can ever *unquestionably* have the semantic value "ego+other." There seems to be but one scene in the play where such is the case, Richard's parting from his wife (V.i). (Here, of course, his "we" is no longer royal.) In the vast majority of cases, apart from those special ones in which the semantic value of Richard's "we" can be confidently determined, the value "ego" seems the more likely.

This situation is very odd. Arguing from the Whorf-Sapir hypothesis,[12] we should say that Richard certainly possesses the concepts "ego" and "other" since he has surface markers ("I" and "you," "he," etc.) for their distinctive realization. The problems arise in attempting to locate the concept "ego+other," which in Richard's mind seems as it were to slide into "ego." One way of resolving the difficulty is to argue as follows: on the one occasion when Richard uses "we" to mean "ego+other," he is in a sense insisting or admitting that such a meaning must be denied him—"we must part" (implicit in V.i.82). We could then understand Richard in this scene as stating one of the limits of his grammar, namely, *(ego+other),[13] and would then read all his other "we"'s as simply "ego."

Such arguments may sound a bit far-fetched, but they do lead in the right direction. For the peculiar semantic rule *(ego+other) becomes comprehensible only, it seems, if we take it as a statement of the excluded middle, that is, $-(\text{ego}+(-\text{ego}))$. This is to say that in Richard's pronouns and presumably in his mind *person* is a single feature, that there is for him only *one* person, with its negation—that *ego* is the *simple negation* of *other*,

---

[12]Its validity for the languages of characters within a single play is a fundamental assumption of this study, one whose propriety the study seeks to demonstrate. The hypothesis, suggested in the work of Edward Sapir and most forcibly advanced by his pupil Benjamin Lee Whorf, is roughly that an individual's comprehension of the world depends on (is affected, limited, or determined by), and therefore can be deduced from, the structure of the language he speaks. See, for example, Whorf, *Language, Thought and Reality*, pp. 212–14.

[13]The asterisk is used in linguistics to designate a form disallowed by the rules of a language. It thus has a meaning quite different from logical negation, for which I here use the minus sign.

and vice versa. We seem here to get at a characteristic of Richard's mind noticed by many readers of the play, one having much to do with his apparent tendency toward solipsism, and with the stark metaphor that begins his soliloquy:

> I have been studying how I may compare
> This prison where I live unto the world;
> And, for because the world is populous
> And here is not a creature but myself,
> I cannot do it. Yet I'll hammer it out.
>   (V.v.1–5)

If the above arguments are valid, we should not expect to find in Richard's speech the alternative realization (to "we") of the semantic combination *ego + other*, namely the conjunction of "I" with any other pronoun or noun. The play thwarts these expectations slightly but not, I think, enough to show us on the wrong track. Perhaps only once is there an unquestionable contradiction—when Richard says that he and Necessity "will keep a league till death" (V.i.21–22).[14]

We mentioned earlier that Richard seems to treat as equivalent or identical the names "King" and "Richard," so that to lose the former is also to lose the latter. But his idea, his conceit, is even more radical. He claims to abandon with his title not only his "name" but also his personal pronoun. When Bolingbroke asks, "Are you contented to resign the crown?" (IV.i.200), Richard replies with puns and paradoxes:

> Ay, no; no, ay; for I must nothing be.
> Therefore no "no," for I resign to thee.
>   (IV.i.201–2)

---

[14]The we-I surface distinction has still not been accounted for. We could go about it in several ways, for instance, by describing "we" and "I" rather oddly perhaps as "ego confident" and "ego unconfident" respectively. Clearly, this is substantially valid if fairly rough; as we have said, Richard's general trend is from the former to the latter. And such a description could be interesting and useful in the consideration of specific passages, especially those in the early parts of the play, where Richard alternates, often repeatedly and in quick succession, between the two forms. Another way to account for the surface distinction, one which is developed below, pp. 30–31, is to see it as marking the distinction between ego-perceived or public ego and ego-perceiving or private ego.

in which the "Ay, no; no, ay" is also "I? no. No I," or perhaps "I?
No. No 'I.' "[15] Richard is saying that if he resigns to Bolingbroke
there is nothing left of him to be content or discontent—nothing
to accept predicates, no token for expression. It would seem that
only in total silence or death can Richard reach the state described in his conceit, and he is in fact soon to be killed. But until
then, at least so long as he continues to talk, his conceit must
remain merely that. And he does continue to talk, notwithstand-
ing that

> my grief lies all within,
> And these external manners of lament
> Are merely shadows to the unseen grief
> That swells with silence in the tortur'd soul.
> (IV.i.295–98)

But as he approaches his death;

> whate'er I be,
> Nor I, nor any man that but man is,
> With nothing shall be pleas'd, till he be eas'd
> With being nothing,
> (V.v.38–41)

he returns to his "No I" conceit, to enlarge upon it pitifully.

The basic form of name giving we have just been considering
consists of a sentence with a personal pronoun or proper noun
as subject, a form of the copula, and a predicate noun. This sort
of utterance is common and important throughout the play, particularly in Richard's speech, as is a similar form, in which both
subject and predicate are common nouns. Both forms can be
included in a basic pattern "X is Y" where the only restrictions
on X and Y are that they both be nouns or pronouns—both be,
in a sense, names. This pattern—call it "S"—shows up in
Richard's talk about himself, his denunciation of others, and in
his characteristic metaphors. We shall return to this form, but
we may note now that it is perfectly suited to the kind of name-
consciousness we have observed in Richard. S-utterances could

[15]Noted by Peter Ure.

in fact be seen as the reduction of language to the manipulation of names. (In this connection it should be noted that sentences of the form "X is Y" in which Y is an adjective are far less prominent in Richard's speech than S-utterances.)[16]

In a sense Richard's apparent successes and his failures alike derive from his tendency to reduce language to a single function, that of naming. His realism and nominalism seem the sides of one coin, mutually exclusive answers to a single yes-or-no question about language. But for Richard, at least, to accept one is irresistibly to call up its antithesis; nor can they be synthesized. And each seems to lead him as badly astray as the other. Saying "Ay, no; no, ay," he is trapped. For him, and to an extent for everyone else in the play, the distinction between *res* and *nomen* appears crucial and yet is repeatedly blurred.[17]

We see thus that "name" is more than thematic, in the usual sense of that word, in *R2*. For in addition to the references to name and the ways in which the plot concerns name, the topic also includes such typical features of the speech action as the grammatical peculiarity of Richard's personal pronouns as well as the form S in which Richard performs his characteristic acts of naming, defining, and the like. This is to say that the theme is reflected in the dramaturgy and vice versa. What Richard says about language, the kind of language he speaks, and the speech acts he performs all seem intimately related, indeed manifestations of a single implied way of conceiving of language.

Literature is full of superficial examples of this sort of relationship between characteristic uses of and references to language—superficial either because the characters are incidental or because, with a major character, the relationship itself is superficial, as with Tamburlaine's talk of threats being manifested

[16]My impression that the one form is "less prominent" than the other in Richard's speech derives from the contexts in which each occurs, and is supported by frequency samplings I have made. The form S, incidentally, is used for (at least) two different kinds of naming: (1) assigning something to a category for which a name exists, and (2) Adamic naming—creating a new name and assigning it.

[17]The metaphor of word, name, utterance as *res* or even person ("Arm, arm, my name") is so pervasive in *R2* that we may become aware of it only through its comparative absence in the following plays, especially in the speech of Hal.

in his threatening. But with Richard we have seen indications of a linguistic unity or integrity of character so deep as practically to be different in kind. This is not only a testament to Shakespeare's characterization: it is also an incentive to further exploration of Richard's speech.

III

Above, the consideration of Richard's talk about name led to analysis of his speech act of naming with its typical grammatical form S, and thence to a consideration of other related speech acts. *Kind of speech act*, that is to say, proved significantly characteristic. Therefore, rather than beginning with a "thematic" body of references to language, I now want to approach Richard's speech action more directly. And since we have seen that there is a unity beneath some superficially unrelated characteristic features, let us attempt to go further into the deep unity of Richard's mind by way of a kind of speech act which is in many respects very different from naming, that is, the act of self-expression.[18]

Political considerations apart,[19] Ross's

> My heart is great, but it must break with silence,
> Ere't be disburdened with a liberal tongue
> (II.i.227–28)

the Duchess of York's

> His words come from his mouth, ours from our breast
> (V.iii.100)

and the Groom of the Stable's

> What my tongue dares not, that my heart shall say
> (V.v.97)

state what might be called a "heart-tongue" theme, the shared

[18]"Self-expression" overlaps both Austin's "behabitives" (*How to Do Things with Words*, pp. 151ff.) and Searle's "expressives" ("A Taxonomy of Illocutionary Acts," pp. 356–58).

[19]Such as the problem of free speech under a powerful government tending toward absolutism. The subject of language in *R2* is susceptible to analysis in political categories which are as germane today as they were for Shakespeare.

imagery of which marks a shared attention to the use of language for expressing emotions, attitudes, and dispositions. As
put by these minor characters the matter is relatively simple—
the tongue either does or does not disburden the heart—and
conventional, so that this little theme might not be worth our
attention if the kind of speech act at issue were not in fact prominently at issue in the play in ways that are neither simple nor
conventional.

Ross disburdening his heart at length to his auditors does
roughly the same thing as the Abbot of Westminster later, who
cautions:

> Before I freely speak my mind herein,
> You shall . . .
> . . . bury mine intents.
>
> (IV,i.327–29)

This is to say that the difference between "heart" (emotions,
etc.) and "mind" (in the abbot's case, "mine intent") is not so
important as the similarity—the fact that "heart" and "mind"
name internal psychological states which may be expressed in
language. The use of language, the kind of speech act, involved,
then, we may roughly term "self-expression."[20] It is important
not only to Ross and the abbot but also to most of the other
characters in the play, especially Richard himself.

Richard's

> grief
> That swells with silence in the tortur'd soul
>
> (IV.i.297–98)

is reminiscent of Ross's remark. But what is simple and conventional with Ross—circumstances will not allow disburdening
the heart—is difficult and peculiar with Richard:

> 'Tis very true, my grief lies all within,
> And these external manners of lament
> Are merely shadows to the unseen grief
> That swells with silence in the tortur'd soul.
>
> (IV.i.295–98)

[20]See above, n. 18.

This is odder than Ure, for instance—"Richard develops the well-loved Shakespearian contrast between *shadow* and *substance*"[21]—will have it. The reason Richard's grief lies "all within" is not, as with Ross, that there are dangers attendant on expressing it. In fact, Richard's grief lying all within *has* been expressed in "external manners of lament." Oddest of all, perhaps, is his "merely"[22]—as though external manners of lament could be anything other than "shadows" of a grief that lies "all within." It is as though he says, "Yes, it's true, the expression of an emotion is only an expression, not the emotion itself," and goes on to say, "therefore it's impossible to express an emotion."

Richard has not so much expressed as paraded his sorrow. Typically, instead of something like "I am sorrowful" (as Hal later says "I am exceeding weary") he says something *about* his sorrow: rather than predicating "grief" of himself he uses a kind of assumed predication.[23] And in this sense, perhaps, we have "manners of lament" rather than actual laments. Such a mode is generally characteristic of Richard; almost always, instead of merely expressing an internal state, he refers to it.

There seems to be a kind of question begging in this mode—a kind of foisting of the recognition of his emotions on those around him; and questions are so begged because they will not bear scrutiny. Richard's mode, then, is an attempt to put across the claim "I have emotions" without the claim's being scrutinized. This too is certainly odd, and the question Richard tries to beg from the other characters is of just the sort we should open further. We may for the moment take his word that his emotion does in some sense lie "all within," and concentrate on his "external manners"—specifically on his consciousness of his external manners, that which is distinctive is the passage.

Richard's consciousness of his external manners is of course implied in the frequent observations that he is vain and theatri-

[21]Peter Ure's note on the passage.

[22]It seems to have the newer meaning "simple, only," rather than the older "completely," but my argument is not affected by which one we prefer.

[23]In grammatical terms, the deep predication has undergone various transformations.

cal, but it is more extreme than such adjectives suggest. Consider, for instance, his

> Down, down I come, like glist'ring Phaeton,
> Wanting the manage of unruly jades,
>   (III.iii.178–79)

lines whose strangeness may have been dulled by familiarity. There is nothing odd about self-aggrandizement, here manifested in Richard's comparing himself with Phaeton, nor about calling attention to oneself and one's actions. What is odd is Richard's saying "Down, down I come" as he comes down, much as a child might say "I'm riding my bicycle" as he rides it. But this oddity complements what we have just been considering. On the one hand, instead of announcing his emotions he refers to them as if they are perfectly apparent; on the other hand, instead of *referring* to an action which is perfectly apparent (as he might by saying something like "My descent is like that of Phaeton," with which we would still retain the elements of self-aggrandizement and attention-getting), he *announces* it.

We have an even more extreme example of Richard's concentration on his external manners when he interrupts Gaunt's warning to say

> A lunatic lean-witted fool,
> Presuming on an ague's privilege,
> Darest with thy frozen admonition
> Make pale our cheek, chasing the royal blood
> With fury from his native residence.
>   (II.i.115–19)

Peculiar as the announcement of his descent was, at least there he knew—could perceive—whereof he spoke. The paling of his cheek, however, is an external manner that (since he has no mirror here) *only* his audience can perceive, that is available exclusively to them. Here, in other words, Richard is thinking absolutely of his "external manners"—thinking of himself merely as perceived by others.

This peculiarity in conceiving of himself is, I think, related to the grammatical peculiarity of the passage discussed earlier, to the fact that in speaking of "our cheek" he uses a first person plural that can only mean "ego." The conjunction of the two peculiarities suggests a further interpretation of Richard's "we" (beyond our provisional "ego confident"), namely *"ego perceived."* And this interpretation seems generally valid: throughout the play generally Richard uses "we" to mean a public identity which exists in the perception, consciousness, and thought of his audience—that-which-is-perceived, as it is perceived, by his public.

This might suggest interpreting his first person singular as "ego not perceived," or "private self," remembering his grief that "lies all within." These terms, however, do not really fit Richard, who through most of the play seems not quite to have a "private self." But if we take Richard's "I" to mean *"ego perceiving"* we have an interpretation that does generally apply. With this reading the I-eye pun becomes resonant (as does, in "I must nothing be," the nothing-noting pun). [24]

In the deposition scene the bringing of the mirror momentarily permits a perfectly closed circuit between Richard's "we"— his face, himself as object of perception—and his "I," himself as perceiver. But this closed circuit cannot last. In these terms Richard is speaking literally when, having destroyed the mirror, he says that his face is "crack'd in an hundred shivers" (IV.i.289), since for his eye it is so, though it remains whole to everyone else. When he abandons his "we," in the last act, and especially in his soliloquy, he is in a sense merely an eye, perceiving much more than before.

What he begins to perceive there is that in neither of the strange entities named by his "we" and "I" is there any scope for will or action—no mechanism for dealing with time. The one can merely receive flattering attention, the other can merely remain in league with grim necessity.

To understand Richard thus helps to explain the peculiar and difficult nature of his "self-expression" and its difference from that of the minor characters discussed. Unlike the abbot, Richard seems to have no "intent," no will to be expressed. Thus his "external manners" are not so much expressions as presentations.

His presentation of himself is manifested not only in his "we"

[24]The pun is almost explicit at IV.i.244–48; it seems implicit in numerous other passages (e.g., I.iii.97–98, I.iii.208–9, II.i.270–71, etc.).

and in specific passages such as his talk of external manners, but also in the fact that his speech action tends to be *explicit,* that his speech contains an unusually large number of performatives. We shall return to this characteristic, but the point here is that "My acts, decrees, and statutes I deny" (IV.i.213), for example, is like his "Down, down I come": in both cases, with the verbal act as with the nonverbal one, Richard is saying what he does *as* he does it—directing attention to the act, presenting it to an audience.

IV

Richard's "Down, down I come" is peculiar for reasons beyond these already discussed.[25] The surface grammar of the verb here is strange. In tense and aspect, it is like that of two of the characteristic kinds of utterance we have already examined, namely the form S (see above, p. 25) and Richard's performatives. With the S-utterances and with the performatives this is the natural, indeed the obligatory, grammar. With "Down, down I come," though the present tense is natural, a different aspect would seem to be more natural (or at least possible), namely, that Richard had said "I am coming down" rather than "I come down." The same peculiarity occurs elsewhere, as when he says "yet one but flatters us" (I.i.25) where "is flattering us" would seem more natural.[26]

[25]Furthermore it is interesting because the Phaeton story is a father-son story; and one of Richard's peculiarities is his general avoidance of conceiving of himself as having had a father (v. above, n. 9). For all his insistence on his right to the crown and on the wrongfulness of Bolingbroke's seizing it, he never talks of succession. This is in part a manifestation of his general refusal to take cognizance of the fact of time or of anything that exists through time (such as the right of succession). It is odd, then, that he should compare himself with the overweening son Phaeton. The simile inadvertently brings out some of the deep contradictions of his thought, which are embodied in the sun-son pun. He would see himself in terms of royal sun imagery without admitting that the sun marks the passage of time.

[26]One could describe "flatters" as an economy of Shakespeare's, since it contains two syllables fewer than "is flattering." Such considerations are real, of course—that is, one feels sure that they could have influenced Shakespeare's word choices. But such a description, if taken as an explanation, is potentially vicious. It eliminates, as it were, the character of Richard. (In Chapter 5 I discuss the viciousness of such "explanations" at some length.) George T. Wright in "The Lyric Present" discusses reasons for and effects of the choice of the simple over the progressive present in lyric poetry.

This usage of Richard's—call it "X"—is not so frequent as S or P (performative), but it does seem characteristic. And, while in certain respects these three kinds of utterance are disparate, the common surface grammar—tense and aspect—marks a similarity in the kinds of speech act for which they are normally used, a similarity which is part of the deep unity of Richard's language.

To get at this unity, let us first consider S and P, the forms in which the surface grammar seems natural. Here the relevant fact about Richard's characteristic form S, whether it be metaphor, analytic statement, definition, self-assertion, self-denial, accusation, or whatever, is that the "tense" of the verb "is" is almost always only a surface phenomenon, since the utterance itself has nothing to do with the present, or with any specific time. The statement S, in other words, is not a description or a report of the present moment. And this fact is marked not only by the "present" tense but also by the aspect: "is," rather than "is being." The performative, P, is a very different class of speech acts, but the same combination of tense and aspect marks the fact that with P no more than with S do we have a report on the present moment: to say "I deny . . ." is not to report that one is denying; it is actually to do it, explicitly.

The reason, then, that Richard's form X seems odd is that he is referring to a fact that is tensed—such as his descent, or someone's flattering him—with a surface grammar that generally marks deep tenselessness. Thus to describe his "X" gets at part of its significance.

The significance can be seen more clearly, I think, in light of the fact that for at least one kind of occasion forms like Richard's "X" are not strange at all, but rather are normal. In plot summaries this occurs when one says "In III.iii, Richard descends to the base court, etc.," wherein the surface tense and aspect of the verb signify that, although an action is being related, it is being conceived as standing outside time, as not locatable in a specific moment of real time, that is, as being eternal. What this suggests as a rationale for Richard's form X is that he conceives of even his own actions as if they stood outside time like events in a story. This too is odd, of course, but it is a conceptual rather than a "merely" linguistic oddity.

Such an account of Richard's "X" not only shows the relation to his characteristic P and S but also fits other facts. For it is in just this way—as a story—that Richard speaks of his life. He does so by implication when in a fit of despair he says

> For God's sake let us sit upon the ground
> And tell sad stories of the death of kings,
> (III.ii.155–56)

and when, parting from his wife, he says

> In winter's tedious nights sit by the fire
> With good old folks, and let them tell thee tales
> Of woeful ages long ago betid;
> And ere thou bid good night, to quite their griefs
> Tell thou the lamentable tale of me
> (V.i.40–44)

this way of thinking is perfectly explicit.

These moments bring us to another feature of Richard's linguistic world inasmuch as they contain references to linguistic *objects* (tales) or *constructs* (rather than, say, linguistic situations, rules, or acts). They represent, further, a special class of linguistic objects in which Richard is absorbed—*literary* objects.

There is in the criticism of the play a large and rather cloudily suggestive body of discussion of Richard as a poet figure—suggestive because it seems to get at something central about Richard, cloudy because the terms and issues remain ill-defined. Part of the problem with this discussion is that "poet" almost always means roughly "lyricist" (a view based mainly on Richard's arialike effusions, which are indeed in a sense lyric). However, Richard's most explicit and direct references to a literary genre are not to the lyric at all, but rather to the narrative, in the examples quoted above; so that for Richard, "poet" as "lyricist" is somewhat out of focus. If we understand "poet" as "constructor of literary objects," though, it accounts for a great deal of Richard's conception and use of language. Even in moments that seem much like lyric poems, such as his soliloquy in Act V, the idea of *constructed* literary objects—for example, comparisons hammered out—is much to the fore.

Yet Richard thinks of himself not only as a constructor of

literary objects, but also as the object constructed and, further, printed, when he says

> I'll read enough
> When I do see the very book indeed
> Where all my sins are writ, and that's myself.
>   (IV.i.273–75)

The problem, then, is that even a generalized view of Richard as a poet figure wrongly suggests kinds of power he does not have and fails to account for his profound powerlessness. And accounting for that powerlessness by calling him a "minor poet" only confuses the matter further: whatever it is that Richard essentially figures, he is surely a major figure of it.

For our purposes, in any case, the truth that is imperfectly stated by calling Richard a poet is that he *conceives of language* poetically, that he typically thinks of language as a material from which to construct literary objects. This applies whether he is hammering out metaphors, speaking of "the lamentable tale of me" or of "the very book . . . that's myself."

This comparatively general characterization is itself a special case of a still more general one based on Richard's tendency to concern himself with linguistic objects, nonliterary as well as literary. We have already seen some of this in the way he speaks of the linguistic object that interests him most, his name, which he conceives very much as an object, seldom giving attention to the act of naming, the relevant institutional and situational rules, and so on. "Name" would in fact seem to comprise the largest part of Richard's concern with verbal objects. And, since we have here an essentially nonliterary object, "literariness" would seem to be of merely subsidiary concern. The underlying logic for this state of affairs is that literariness for Richard is simply an intensification of verbal object-ness: arranged in a couplet or written on a page, a linguistic object gains additional properties.

"Name" is by no means the only nonliterary verbal object to concern Richard. When he says to Mowbray

> The hopeless word of "never to return"
> Breathe I against thee
>   (I.iii.152–53)

he talks of speech virtually as the projection of an object by breath. This is something of a paradigm which influences our interpretation of a number of his later remarks, such as

> After our sentence plaining comes too late,
> (I.iii.175)

> Darest with thy frozen admonition
> Make pale our cheek,
> (II.i.117–18)

> Mock not my senseless conjuration, lords,
> (III.ii.23)

> Speak to his gentle hearing kind commends,
> (III.iii.126)

> this tongue of mine,
> That laid the sentence of dread banishment
> On yon proud man.
> (III.iii.133–35)

Nouns that name *non*verbal acts (e.g., "murder") normally are used to refer simply to the act, with such certain exceptional classes as the use of a noun like "painting" to name either the act or the resulting product of the act. But with nouns that name *verbal* acts, such as Richard's "sentence," "admonition," "conjuration," there is a special ambiguity between (1) the illocutionary act and (2) the utterance or verbal object in which the act is performed—which is not at all the same as the act-product ambiguity. There are alternate unambiguous forms, of course—for example, "conjuring," "admonishing," and others—to refer to the act, and periphrases like "words of admonition" to refer to the verbal object, but Richard does not normally use them. In the light of what we have already seen, his predilection for the ambiguous forms suggests that even when he seems officially to be talking about verbal *acts* he is in some sense still talking about verbal *objects*. With "frozen admonition" the adjective reinforces this suggestion. And beneath "speak . . . kind commends" lies the same model of the exhaled object as in "word . . . Breathe I against you," in spite of Richard's use of the verb "speak."

Richard's verbal objects also have to do with the nature of his "self-expression" discussed above (section III). An expression and an expressing are not the same; and for Richard language is a medium for constructing expressions rather than for expressing. But once constructed the object is objective and not subjective—is tied to the self even less than "external manners." From time to time, as when he ends his farewell to his wife with "Once more, adieu; the rest let sorrow say" (V.ii. 102), he talks as if there were adequate words of the self which, by his odd logic, in order to be authentic must not be uttered. Yet if they remain private they cannot be known even to the self. A solution would be to have the words of the heart discovered by someone else; and there may be a suggestion of this when Richard's queen asks him "Hath Bolingbroke . . . been in thy heart?" (V.i. 27–28).[27]

V

In the previous sections we have been trying to describe Richard's conception of language, or his linguistic "world," by moving back and forth between (1) what he says about language, (2) the kind of language he uses, and (3) the kind of speech acts he performs. This is approximately to say that we have been engaged in the deductive analysis of (1) theme, (2) style, and (3) local dramaturgy. Since categories (1) and (2), having been attended to in the criticism of the play (especially in this century) much more than (3), are much the more familiar, I have generally moved from (1) and (2) to (3), placing the latter in the context of the former and dealing with features of (3) that have fairly direct correlates in (1) and (2). Now, however, I want to conclude the intensive discussion of Richard by concentrating on category (3), by considering a feature of Richard's speech action (or, alternatively, Shakespeare's local dramaturgy) which does not have such direct thematic or stylistic correlates and yet, in ways I shall try to show, is characteristic and therefore related to what we have seen thus far.

[27]Such an account of the relation between Richard's concern with verbal objects and his problem of self is supported by the fact that at one moment in the York-Aumerle subplot there is a kind of allegorical embodiment of these matters. Here the words of the heart are an actual document which Aumerle resists showing, and which York insists on seeing until he finally *"plucks it out of his bosom and reads it"* (S. D., V.ii.71; *Qq; Snatches it, F*).

Richard's

> I have been studying how I may compare
> This prison where I live unto the world;
> And, for because the world is populous
> And here is not a creature but myself,
> I cannot do it. Yet I'll hammer it out
>
> (V.v.1–5ff.)

is, as we have seen, an example of his characteristic of constructing an object in the medium of language, in this case a poemlike
object; and the frequency of his construction of such objects
gives rise to the ultimately unsatisfactory view of him as a figure
of the (lyric) poet.

Now this speech is poemlike for reasons beyond those having
to do with the idea of verbal objects. Beyond such features as the
forced and extended comparison, the kind of thought displayed,
the logical structure, and so on, the speech is like one of
Shakespeare's sonnets in that the *direction of address* is unchang-
ing and ambiguous between the speaker's talking to himself or
to the work's audience. In dramatic terms, that is, the speech is
soliloquy. Commentators have noted that on a number of occasions Richard hammers out comparisons and develops metaphors lengthily and elaborately. But what has not, I believe,
been noticed is that with regard to direction of address as well,
an unusually large portion resembles "I have been studying
how I may compare. . . ." That is, an unusually large portion of
Richard's speech is formally like soliloquy, even though the
speech in Act V is the only "true" example.

Soliloquy is a familiar device of Elizabethan drama, and
Shakespearean soliloquy has been examined by a number of
scholars.[28] Their studies are largely devoted to distinguishing
types or uses of soliloquy, and they take the basic idea of soliloquy as a given. Yet the formal characteristics—the linguistic
manifestations—that distinguish soliloquy from other speech
are not immediately obvious.

If no character other than the speaker is onstage, nor any is

---

[28]For commentary on Shakespeare's soliloquies, in addition to sections of
works on dramaturgy, see Morris LeRoy Arnold, *The Soliloquies of Shakespeare*
and Wolfgang Clemen, *Shakespeare's Soliloquies*.

presumed earshot offstage, then we of course have soliloquy
and of the most familiar kind. But though this situational
criterion is a sufficient condition it is not necessary. For even
with other characters onstage there can be soliloquy —
in the form of an aside, for instance, or a case in which the
speaker *believes* himself to be alone.[29] What all these sorts of
soliloquies share is their not being *addressed* to other characters
onstage or offstage within earshot (this is a necessary condition,
but not a sufficient one — there are prologues, etc., which we do
not call soliloquy). And in spite of the fact that with a given
speech we usually know whether or not it is so addressed, *how*
we know this is a complicated matter.

The ways we determine that a speech *is* directed toward an
onstage addressee (and thus is not soliloquy) are several. The
most complex involves communication of information. If B's re-
sponse, or other subsequent developments, show that A passed
and intended to pass information to B, then we know that A has
addressed B. This is an external (to the utterance) or situational
criterion for address, roughly analogous to the situational
criteria for soliloquy. The other ways of determining that A has
addressed someone onstage, and thus is not soliloquizing, are
simpler and have to do with the form of the speech in question — that is, they are internal manifestations of address. A
vocative, for instance, names the addressee. The use of a second
person pronoun also establishes the direction of address, since
the "second person" is simply the person addressed. The case is
similar with an "inclusive" first person plural.[30] Finally, the imperative or the interrogative (itself a kind of imperative) mood
can manifest address: one commands or interrogates a certain
person.[31]

In soliloquy or aside, then, all these features are necessarily
absent, and, of course, they are absent from Richard's soliloquy
in Act V. But what is interesting is that in *all* of his speech these

[29]Such as the bravura quadruply-nested, eavesdropped soliloquies in *Love's
Labour's Lost* (IV.iii).
[30]The "inclusive 'we'" includes the addressee; the "exclusive 'we'" does not.
[31]Complicated as this is, it is still something of an idealization. One could
imagine an *aside* in which A spoke of B with a second person — for example,
"You'll regret that." I think that such exceptions are fairly rare and can be dealt
with by slight modifications of the account given here.

features tend to be absent. When in a single passage they are all lacking we have something formally indistinguishable from soliloquy of the aside kind, that is, speech which could actually be staged as soliloquy. That this is not done must be a result of stage tradition and the way we instinctively conceive of drama, taking a speech as addressed to someone onstage if at all possible. A speech lacking some but not all of these features could not be staged as soliloquy, of course. But the more these features are absent the more the speech becomes formally like soliloquy, and also, as mentioned earlier, like lyric or narrative.

The best way to summarize this, I believe, is to posit *direction of address* as a feature of speech acts, specifically of illocutionary acts, which is manifested in the other features discussed;[32] and to say that Richard's speech action characteristically and distinctively tends toward the unmarked nonspecific direction of address typical of nondramatic literary genres and, within drama, of soliloquy.

The significance of this characteristic of Richard's is suggested by the fact that its formal manifestation overlaps certain features of his language already found to be significant for other reasons. We have seen, for instance, that the absence of the inclusive "we," which is one manifestation of his peculiar direction of address, is also significant as a manifestation of his conceiving of himself as either ego-perceiving or ego-perceived—absolutely public or absolutely private—or both. This coupled with what we have already noted about conventional uses of unmarked direction of address, suggests part of the significance of that direction of address in Richard's speech; normal uses of this direction of address are in the "absolutely private" speech of dramatic soliloquy and the "absolutely public" language of lyrics or narratives intended for publication, that is, directed toward a general nonspecific public.[33]

[32]The redundancy of "direction of address" is regrettable but necessary, I think: "address" does not make the point explicit enough. The feature is touched on little, if at all, in Austin and Searle.

[33]With the lyric, unmarked direction of address often permits *both* the absolute privacy involved in the sense of the poet's speaking to no ear but his own—soliloquizing, as it were—*and* the absolute publicity of the poem's being addressed to a general unspecified audience. In drama we have something roughly analogous. Most soliloquies seem to be strictly private speech, but sometimes, especially with aside, there is an ambiguity between (1) private

In Richard's speech unmarked direction of address functions mainly, I think, to give a soliloquylike quality that is delicate and yet so pervasive that many readers familiar with the play would be surprised to be told that Richard has only one ("true") soliloquy. Because of this general quality that last soliloquy has the rightness and inevitability of something toward which Richard has been tending all along; for, throughout the play, his unmarked direction of address has produced the subtle effect of his talking to himself even when he appears to be talking to others. His tendency toward soliloquy manifests his tending toward solipsism and isolation. Yet at the same time his unmarked direction of address manifests his completely public quality—the sense of him as sheer appearance, existing for, and only in the consciousness of, a general audience. In this respect his direction of address is like his performatives.

This is to show the relationship of Richard's direction of address to what we have noticed before, but it is also to imply a further characteristic which we have not yet described. For, inasmuch as his speech is addressed to himself and/or a general audience, it is *not* addressed to any specific hearer. His peculiar direction of address, that is, tends to preclude his conversing—verbally engaging or interacting—with anyone. What we thus see locally, in the dramaturgy of speech action, is of course also apparent in the plot as a whole, in his not quite engaging Bolingbroke, in the fact that there is no real agon between them. "Passive," the usual term for this quality of Richard's, describes his not acting on others, but, by making him seem acted upon, it obscures his isolation. A better grammatical term might be "reflexive."

Since I have pressed the direction of address (as well as other features) of Richard's speech action rather hard, I should, before

---

speech and (2) that addressed to the general public of the play's audience. Also in drama, with prologue, chorus, and so on, we have something situationally like soliloquy—a single character onstage—which is absolutely public, that is, addressed entirely to the general public of the play's audience, in which one could imagine unmarked direction of address (though, as it happens, Shakespeare's prologues typically have direction of address marked with second person pronouns). In narrative, unmarked direction of address seems almost always exclusively to manifest address to a general public; though with some recent narrative influenced by stream-of-consciousness, unmarked direction of address has the same public-private quality as lyric.

turning again to the action of the whole play, deal with a possible objection: that this feature of Richard's speech is merely a symptom of the immaturity of Shakespeare's dramaturgy since, after all, many of the characters in Marlowe, for instance, speak in soliloquylike arias without much interaction. What I have described *may* reflect an immaturity of technique—that Shakespeare *may* not yet have had the possibility of making Richard engage in verbal interaction more than he does. However, because of the pervasive concentration on problems of language and speech, this feature is, I would claim, significant and functional in *R2* as it would not be in a play of Marlowe's. Richard's direction of address is an example of a fairly radical economy that begins to appear in Shakespeare's work at about this period: the economy of making the very limitations of the art contribute to its aesthetic unity.

VI

In the preceding sections I have been trying to demonstrate a thematic, stylistic, and dramaturgical unity which may be called Richard's linguistic world or conception of language (bearing in mind that "Richard" here is the embodiment of that conception rather than a verisimilar representation who happens to think in a certain way, and letting "conception" mean "way of conceiving" rather than something narrower like "definition"). One might say, then, that the overall action of the play is the decline and fall of this conception of language, of Richard's linguistic world.

James L. Calderwood, in the last chapter of *Shakespearean Metadrama*, in fact says approximately this, and very persuasively. In spite of differences in approach his view of Richard seems close to mine[34]; and, though he does not deal with the play as part of a larger unit, he does use two of the summary metaphors I shall be using for the action of the entire tetralogy. Regarding the analogue of the Fall, Calderwood suggests that Richard's fall is from a state of converse with God and of the divinely sanctioned and absolute power to assign names.[35]

[34]Calderwood is more theological and "metadramatic"; I am more linguistic and linguistic-philosophical.

[35]*Shakespearean Metadrama*, pp. 173, 175.

Much more extensively he shows that Tillyard's historical metaphor for the action of *R2*—the end of the Middle Ages—summarizes much of Richard's conception of language as magical, ceremonial, and part of a divinely authorized hierarchy, and his conception of his own speech as carrying an authority like that of a medieval pope.[36] In terms of these metaphors Calderwood's account is, I think, basically in accord with the above discussion.

However, Calderwood's view of the movement summarized by these metaphors as "The Fall of Speech" (the title of his chapter on the play) seems, like other recent commentary, to obscure matters by viewing the entire action from Richard's standpoint. What falls, after all, is only *Richard's* speech—his conception of language—not, as he would have it, "Speech" itself. And what rises is Bolingbroke's speech.

One can understand the customary view of Bolingbroke, set forth by Calderwood and other commentators, that his "intentions are communicated not by speech but by the blunt expressiveness of twenty thousand armed bodies,"[37] the view that the force of his speech "derives from the fact that his words are laden with money,"[38] that, in terms of the historical metaphor, Bolingbroke is a Renaissance prince so concerned with "manipulative efficiency"[39] achieved through nonverbal instruments like money and armies that he brings to the throne no noteworthy conception of language or linguistic world. Certainly, Richard is so obsessed with his language, and his opposite, Bolingbroke, the "silent king," is so reticent—even negative—that it is tempting to see the action simply as "the fall of speech" followed by a kind of silence.

Nevertheless, it does seem possible and indeed right to see the entire action—Richard's fall *and* Bolingbroke's rise—in terms of conceptions and uses of language. Long before Bolingbroke's accession his linguistic world is foreshadowed, or at least certain features of it, so that from early on there is present a dynamic in the way the play is "about" language.

This foreshadowing occurs in one of the play's most memora-

[36]*Ibid.*, p. 169.
[37]*Ibid.*, p. 172.
[38]*Ibid.*, p. 184.
[39]*Ibid.*, p. 182.

ble speeches about language, one which we have not yet discussed,[40] Mowbray's lament at being banished:

> The language I have learnt these forty years,
> My native English, now I must forgo,
> And now my tongue's use is to me no more
> Than an unstrung viol or a harp . . .
> . . . .
> What is thy sentence then but speechless death,
> Which robs my tongue from breathing native breath?
> (I.iii.159–73)

The length and eloquence of this speech, in contrast with Bolingbroke's clipped

> Your will be done; this must my comfort be,
> That sun that warms you here, shall shine on me,
> And those his golden beams to you here lent
> Shall point on me and gild my banishment
> (I.iii.144–47)

is usually accounted for by Mowbray's having expected Richard to favor him. Yet surely the *topic* of the speech—that the only hardship Mowbray foresees in banishment is having to learn French—is more surprising than typical editorial comment would lead one to believe.[41]

The significance of the speech becomes clearer in light of the configuration formed by Mowbray, Bolingbroke, and Richard at this moment in the play. As suggested earlier, there is with Richard a kind of equation between his consciousness and the nation, so that banishing the two men is his way of putting them both out of his mind. Bolingbroke's reply to the sentence (which is also a little surprising, since he refuses to be comforted by it when his father says almost the same thing to him at the end of the scene) serves, then, as a warning: "there are realities outside your limited consciousness; you are not all-seeing like the sun;

---

[40]And one which Calderwood notably fails to take account of.

[41]Ure, for instance, mentions that "*tongue* is both the physical organ and the 'native language' which it speaks: both useless instruments," glosses several words, and ends with "Mowbray is saying that he is too advanced in years to learn to speak as a baby learns from his nurse." Nor can one be satisfied with the reductive if true "explanation" that this is an example of the importance of language in the play.

though banished, I continue to exist" and furthermore, perhaps, by way of the sun-royalty equation, "I am still powerful, and potentially a king." This warning Richard apparently ignores, for he immediately turns to sentence Mowbray.

It is in the light of these facts, I think, that Mowbray's lament should be seen. He is not issuing a warning to his king, of course. He is more submissive than Bolingbroke, and Richard's description of the speech as "plaining" (l. 175) seems accurate at least with respect to Mowbray's conscious intention. However, there has been an insistent parallelism between Mowbray and Bolingbroke up to this point, and I suggest that it continues to obtain here, that in Mowbray's speech, too, there is an element of (unintended) warning for Richard, a warning which Richard no more recognizes than he does Bolingbroke's. As with the latter's speech the warning note is sounded by reference to facts beyond Richard's ken; and in this case the facts are linguistic.

Specifically, what Richard should hearken to in Mowbray's speech is that there are a variety of languages: that the king's is merely "English" and not universal. That Mowbray finds this fact difficult and painful to face shows the limits of Richard's linguistic world. Having been Richard's lieutenant means having assented to Richard's conception of language. And what is difficult for Mowbray to face is simply not faced at all by Richard. Not here nor anywhere else in the play does Richard seem aware of the fact of the variety of languages.

That he should be not aware of that fact is consistent with what we have already noted about him—his abstract and absolutist conception of language, his concern with problems related to realism and nominalism, problems, in other words, which in their very formulation almost require the ignoring of differences between languages. There are of course any number of facts about language which Richard ignores. But the importance of *this* fact is that it is stated positively so that we do not have an omission—a silence around Richard's speech—but rather a suggested alternative, an intimation of a linguistic "world" of facts and problems involving the variety of languages. And, though Richard is not cognizant of it, this "world" exists in the play.

Thus Mowbray's lament provides a basis for evaluating the

process or dynamic of the entire action of the play. What falls is not "Speech" but speech in a language mistakenly supposed to be universal; and what begins to rise in this play and continues to rise throughout the tetralogy is the world of differing languages. This aspect of the general action suggests that the medieval-Renaissance summary metaphor is apropos in ways beyond those noted by Tillyard and Calderwood: the play enacts a transition from something like the medieval universality of Latin to the Renaissance proliferation and predominance of the European vernaculars.

This aspect of the subject of language in the tetralogy is important enough for a separate summary metaphor. The obvious choice, one whose suitability will be demonstrated further in later chapters, is the Babel story. It is useful not only because it constitutes the most familiar rationalization of the fact of the variety of languages (there seems to be virtually no attempt in the classical tradition to account for this fact[42]), but also because of its morality—the universal tongue and the getting or making of a name, like the tower itself, are kinds of overweening for which the proliferation of languages is a punishment. From the moral standpoint, then, the Babel story is analogous to that of the Fall. And in the tetralogy the fact of the variety of languages seems like a symptom of a fallen world.[43]

This is true even in *R2*. In Mowbray's lament, the first appearance of the Babel theme, the fact of the variety of languages is merely a part of what Richard ignores. But later, when he has fallen and Bolingbroke has become king, in the scene in which the Duke and Duchess of York quarrel with each other before Bolingbroke over the fate of their son Aumerle—

> *Duchess.* No word like "pardon" for kings' mouths so meet.

[42]This is true, as far as I can tell, of the Greek mythological system; and it is also true of later philosophy of language, about which Otto Jespersen says

> Endless discussions were carried on . . . as we see particularly from Plato's *Kratylos,* and no very definite result was arrived at, nor could any be expected so long as one language only formed the basis of the discussion.
> (*Language,* p. 19)

[43]For the Babel story (Gen. 11:1–9), see Introduction, n. 4. A good recent commentary on the Babel story is in Gerhard Von Rand, *Genesis.*

York. Speak it in French, king, say "Pardonne moy."
Duchess. Dost thou teach pardon pardon to destroy?
Ah, my sour husband, my hard-hearted lord,
That sets the word itself against the word!
Speak "pardon" as 'tis current in our land.
                              (V.iii.116–121)

—the fact of the variety of languages begins increasingly to seem an unfortunate symptom of the world that has resulted from Richard's overthrow.

VII

In conclusion, then, *R2* represents an opposition between two linguistic worlds. On the one hand there is Richard's univocal, unilingual, absolutist world of nomenclature, ceremonial performatives, and others of the features noted above. On the other hand there is Bolingbroke's world of tongues and silence, a way of conceiving of language whose ramifications, merely suggested in *R2*, are developed in the *H4* plays.

In *R2* the culmination of this opposition is Richard's death, an event which reflects both linguistic worlds. The play, which began with Richard's discovery that issuing a command is not the same as having it obeyed, ends with his murder as a result of Exton's taking Bolingbroke's "very words" (V.iv.3) as a command which he hastens to obey. The murder is in a sense caused by Bolingbroke's silence—in this case the lack of explicitness that allows (or encourages) Exton to interpret " 'Have I no friend?' " as "urging" (V.iv.4–5) and, when the murder is done, to claim "From your own mouth, my lord, did I this deed" (V.vi.37). In the large design of the tetralogy the mechanics of the murder are a foretaste of the linguistic world that results from Richard's fall, a world of linguistic problems (such as interpretation and responsibility) different in kind from Richard's.

But even considered on its own Richard's fall has peculiarities that manifest his conception of language: he falls from a linguistic Eden that never existed except in his own mind. And in a sense his fall consists of the opening of his eyes not only to the events he is caught up in but also to what his own language and thought entail.

In the early and middle scenes, understanding is forced on him in bits and pieces against which he cries out with questions like "Is not the king's name twenty thousand names?" But in Act V, with Bolingbroke on the throne, Richard's comprehension grows, and in two speeches he gives summary assessments of his situation.

The first of these is his farewell to his wife —

> Learn, good soul,
> To think our former state a happy dream;
> From which awak'd, the truth of what we are
> Shows us but this. I am sworn brother, sweet,
> To grim Necessity, and he and I
> Will keep a league till death.
>
> (V.i.17–22)

This could stand as a summary of much of what we have noted about Richard.[44] But in this version of "the truth of what we are" characteristic limitations are also apparent. Richard has not yet completely awakened; the happy dream has become grim, but it is still a dream. What he has yet to see is that his "Necessity" and "dream" are not opposites at all, but rather that "Necessity" is a part of his dream, whether it be happy as when he supposes that his name of king is a necessary adjunct, or grim, as here. And the context of the speech heightens the irony of his growing but still limited perception. For in this scene, just as he is swearing his league to Necessity, reality for once seems magically subject to his word: after he twice urges his queen to go to France, Northumberland enters with an order from Bolingbroke that she be taken there.

It is after this last audience has departed that Richard, alone in his cell, reaches the final stage of understanding his situation and, realizing that he has been generally in error, summarizes the matter more comprehensively, accurately, and as it were nakedly than in his farewell to his wife.

There may be in the soliloquy some distant allusion to the variety of languages when with

[44]Richard's "Necessity" seems something more like logical implication than causation. His favored form S, for instance, is a kind of logical equation — obviously so when it is a definition, and also, though less obviously, when it is a metaphor.

>   do set the word itself
>   Against the word
>   (V.v.13–14)

Richard echoes the Duchess of York's description of her husband's French.[45] But, by and large, this aspect of what has been
excluded from his conception of language never comes home to
him. What he does recognize in his soliloquy is related less to
the Babel analogue than to the Fall and the Renaissance. For he
comes closest to a summary description of his flaw in the line "I
wasted time, and now doth time waste me" (V.v.49). The general accuracy of this observation is clear. Richard has wasted
time in disastrously failing to seize the day (as at III.ii.64ff.). He
has tried disastrously to waste (destroy) time in the action
against which York warns:

>   Take Herford's rights away, and take from time
>   His charters, and his customary rights;
>   Let not to-morrow then ensue to-day;
>   Be not thyself. For how art thou a king
>   But by fair sequence and succession?
>   (II.i.195–99)

in which the very imagery amplifies one of the play's large
ironies—the fact that the sun, the central symbol of royalty, is
itself man's essential marker for the passage of time (and,
through the sun-son pun, suggests the Shakespearean *topos*
of procreation as one of man's essential ways of transcending time).

But Richard's "I wasted time" is also a satisfactory summary
description of his linguistic world and its fall. For virtually
everything we have noted about him implies a failure—inability
or refusal—to admit time into the scope of his attention.

The rationalist philosopher in him would deal in eternal verities, in a logical attack on the idea of reference, neglecting such
temporal matters as the variety of occasions, circumstances, and
languages in which names are given, taken, accepted, manipu-
lated, altered. The "poet" conceives of language as a material in
which to construct timeless objects—especially names—rather

---

[45] At V.iii.120. But metrical irregularity in Richard's speech suggests the possibility that the repetition is a textual error.

than a medium in which acts are performed. Characteristically, Richard's present "tense" is a surface feature of the syntax which marks a deep tenselessness, both in his form S and in his performatives; and he uses the same surface grammar in his form "X" ("Down, down I come") so as to suggest that this deep tenselessness extends even to utterances ostensibly meant as tensed. And his "we" and/or "I"—merely public appearance and/or merely private perception—lacks any mechanism for will or action in time.

Richard's ignoring and thus wasting "fair sequence and succession" is also apparent in the nature of his speech action. Both the soliloquylike nature of his "dialogue" and its ceremonial explicitness manifest an avoidance of using language for interaction and they isolate him from his interlocutors so that his speech cannot have direct consequences.

We have seen ways in which Bolingbroke's linguistic world is opposed to Richard's, and in the following chapters I will show specifically that his speech action is unlike Richard's. But perhaps the atemporal quality of Richard's speech action can best be brought into a final focus by a comparison with that of his more distant opposite, Hal. For the speech action of the two men is strikingly different.

Austin's provisional taxonomy of illocutionary force proves beautifully helpful here. Richard's speech acts tend to be of the kind Austin calls "exercitives":

> An exercitive is the giving of a decision in favour of or against a certain course of action, or advocacy of it. It is a decision that something is to be so, as opposed to an estimate that it is so; it is an award as opposed to an assessment; it is a sentence as opposed to a verdict.
> (*How to do Things with Words*, p. 154)

Of the examples Austin gives of this sort of speech act, those particularly noteworthy in Richard include name, appoint, order, command, sentence, proclaim, announce, and resign. Hal, on the other hand, even when he becomes king, characteristically performs "commissives": "The whole point of a commissive is to commit the speaker to a certain course of action" (p. 156).

Here the basic example is the promise or the declaration of intention, which is characteristic of Hal.

The point, then, is that, while Hal's commissives (pointing to a time other than that of the utterance) exhibit in themselves an awareness of the fact of time, quite the reverse is the case with Richard's exercitives, which have the simultaneity or "token reflexivity" that pertains to all speech acts when they are performatives. Exercitives command that a state or situation be, and in a sense take effect immediately or not at all. For Richard, the example par excellence is official naming, in which ideas of time and intention seem irrelevant. Richard performs this sort of act naturally in his legislative and executive role of king, performs it there as if *on* his realm. But he also performs it, when he is no longer king, on himself, bizarrely and unnaturally: "I must nothing be."

Thus Richard's "I wasted time, and now doth time waste me" embraces much of what we have observed about his language; and it is certainly as close as Richard himself comes to a comprehensive description of his linguistic world. Even this description, however, has limitations which will become clearer as, in the following chapters, the other Lancastrian plays provide a context for further definition and summary of what has here been noted about *R2*.

CHAPTER TWO

❋ *1 Henry IV*

1 Henry IV, unlike the other three plays of the tetralogy, has neither a single major interaction between two characters extending throughout the play (as with Falstaff and the Lord Chief Justice in *2H4*) nor a single character whose speech dominates (as with Richard in *R2* and Hal in *H5*). The pattern of interactions here is thus more complex. I have tried to do justice to that complexity in the format of this chapter, first attempting a description of the distinctive "world" of conceptions and uses of language in the play with (I) a fairly wide-ranging survey of the matter followed by (II) an intensive analysis of a distinctive feature of the play's verbal interaction, the feature of "control." Then (III–VI) the play's four central characters are considered individually. Within each of these I move generally from the thematic to the dramaturgical: from what the character says *about* language, or what is said about his language, to what seems distinctive about his use of language in speech action. Of these four characters, I give special attention to Henry, the one who seems to have been most slighted in the criticism; I spend less time with Hal and Falstaff who will be considered extensively in later chapters. Finally (VII), I recapitulate and summarize.

I

Some of the ways in which the speech action and conceptions of language in *1H4* are Renaissance as opposed to the medieval of *R2* have been commented on by scholars. Tillyard's discussions are famous;[1] Eric La Guardia finds that after the "ceremonial" language of *R2* the language of *1H4* is "practical."[2] Both the Renaissance predominance of the vulgar tongues and the proliferation of tongues in the Babel story are suggested by the difficulty of Lord and Lady Mortimer:

> *Mortimer.* This is the deadly spite that angers me, My
>   wife can speak no English, I no Welsh
>   (III.i.186–88)

and by the fact that there is conversation in Welsh on stage.

The summary metaphor of the Fall is alluded to when Hal says

> I am now of all humours that have showed themselves
> humours since the old days of goodman Adam to the
> pupil age of this present twelve o'clock at midnight.
>   (II.iv.90–92)

The tone of this is significant and fairly typical of *1H4*. Just as Adam can be mentioned lightly here, without much sense of the seriousness of the effects of the Fall, so, as when Hotspur says

> In Richard's time—what do you call the place?
> A plague upon it, it is in Gloucestershire
>   (I.iii.239–40)

Richard can be mentioned easily and straightforwardly, without the magnitude of the effects of his fall being felt. It is as if, coming before the fuller realization of loss in *2H4*, this play presents an immediate vigor released by the breaking of the charmed circle of Richard's rule. The release and the vigor are notably apparent in the comedy of inconsequential talk and in the interruption of the verse with prose. And we can also see the change in the treatment of thematic topics involving language and speech action.

A good case in point is the topic of naming. In *R2* it was a focus of Richard's realist-nominalist conflict, and in his linguistic absolutism the validity of names was a test case for the general validity of language; similarly, name as title was a test case for

[1]E. M. W. Tillyard, *Shakespeare's History Plays.*
[2]Eric La Guardia, "Ceremony and History."

the entire social order. But in *1H4* this way of thinking has largely subsided. We find relatively little of it even with Henry, whom we might most expect to express it, and who indeed did express it notably in *R2*. And what the other characters say about name shows new attitudes and preconceptions that were not present in *R2*. Hotspur, for instance, *forgets* names, as in the lines quoted above (p. 53), and so does Falstaff:

> he of Wales that . . . swore the devil his true liegeman
> upon the cross of a Welsh hook—what a plague call
> you him?
>
> (II.iv.332–35)

Hal coins names for Falstaff (whose own name, of course, has changed from "Oldcastle"): "call in Ribs, call in Tallow." These and other such moments exemplify a midway stage in the movement from *R2*, where only "sick men play with their names" and where names are too important to be forgotten, to *2H4*, where "what a disgrace it is to me that I remember your name" (II.ii.12–13) and where, with Shallow, Silence, Tearsheet, Mouldy, and Wart, even playing with names grows pointless.

The topic of names is shallower in *1H4* than in *R2*; yet it is also broader since more than in *R2* it extends beyond personal titles and proper names to common nouns. Gadshill is using a frequently cited example of the common noun, from a grammar,[3] when he points out that *"homo* is a common name to all men" (II.i.93). And the comically superfluous Latin makes his remark doubly typical of the concern with name in *1H4*: to use a "common name" is not only to denote a particular language but also to use it, and in *1H4* the fact of the variety of languages becomes involved with the concept of name (as it was not in *R2*). Douglas boasts

> there is not such a word
> Spoke of in Scotland as this term of fear,
> (IV.i.84–85)

claiming that his countrymen have no "common name" for fear. Hal is pleased to have learned " 'dyeing scarlet,' " the drawers'

---

[3]Lily and Colet, *Shorte Introduction of Grammar* (1549), cited by Humphreys in his note on the passage.

term for "drinking deep" (II.iv.15). Using the Babel metaphor one might say that with the fall of the tower, the absolute theoretical questions about name have given way to practical questions of dealing with the proliferated tongues—to such questions as how to translate names.

Hal touches on almost all of this, albeit humorously, in the speech (II.iv.4–33) in which he describes to Poins his sounding "the very base-string of humility" in company with "a leash of drawers" and then proposes a trick on the drawer Francis. Hal says that the drawers

> call drinking deep "dyeing scarlet," and when you
> breathe in your watering, they cry "Hem!" and bid you
> "Play it off!" To conclude, I am so good a proficient in
> one quarter of an hour that I can drink with any tinker
> in his own language during my life,
>
> (II.iv.15–19)

thus bringing up the variety of tongues and showing the new kind of importance assumed by naming—calling—in that context. Variety of tongues is also implicit in Hal's mention of Francis "that never spake other English in his life than 'Eight shillings and sixpence,' and 'you are welcome.'" For this is one of the few times in the early part of the tetralogy that the tongue spoken by most of the characters is named and so placed as one of many. And Hal here also subsumes both common names ("'dyeing scarlet'") and proper names—

> I . . . can call them all by their christen names, as Tom,
> Dick and Francis
>
> (II.iv.6–8)

—under the one rubric of calling.

Furthermore Hal in the same speech makes a kind of subterranean or implied pun on "call" which signals a new development in the topic of naming. After using the word as above, he goes on to use it as "summon" in the trick he proposes to play on Francis:

> do thou never leave calling "Francis!", that his tale to
> me may be nothing but "Anon."
>
> (II.iv.31–33)

The trick is of course performed; and the kind of calling involved is later showcased in

> *Glendower.* I can call spirits from the vasty deep.
> *Hotspur.* Why, so can I, or so can any man,
> But will they come when you do call for them?
>   (III.i.50–52)

I think that Shakespeare's emphasis on this kind of "calling" has several importances. In the first place it is connected with the vocatives which are more prominent in this play than in *R2*. Indeed the vocative embodies the pun on "call," being at once a kind of terming or naming and also a kind of summoning, a summoning to attend. And, as manifestations of direction of address and, more, of the fact of verbal interaction, the vocatives of *1H4* are symptoms of the world that has resulted from the end of the domination of Richard's absolutist tongue. Furthermore, calling as summoning seems important in the way it differs from the calling as dubbing that is prevalent in *R2*. For the two kinds of calling belong to two large classes of speech acts which seem fairly typical of the two plays. Dubbing is like pronouncing, defining, asserting, sentencing, and a number of other speech acts important in *R2* in that the act itself involves little if any conceptual reference to time, and also in that there is no essential reference to any kind of action. Summoning, on the other hand, is like threatening, promising, urging, and a number of other speech acts important in *1H4* in that the act involves essential conceptual reference to time and action.[4]

A further feature of the topic of name in *1H4* that distinguishes the play from *R2* is touched on by Hal in his "leash of drawers" speech when he says

> I tell thee, Ned, thou hast lost much honour that thou
> wert not with me in this action; but, sweet Ned—to
> sweeten which name of Ned I give thee this
> pennyworth of sugar.
>   (II.iv.19–23)

In *R2* the social dimension of name concerned the authority of "the name of king" and other hereditary titles such as "Duke of Lancaster." But in *1H4* "name" more often connotes honor,

---

[4]In *2H4* (II.iv.98,100) the two uses of "call" appear again in quick succession, but by then the emphasis has shifted again; the clash between the two meanings receives no emphasis and may pass unnoticed.

fame, reputation. Most of this conception centers about the character whose most familiar name—"Hotspur"—is itself an example of nomenclature which has nothing to do with inheritance, but rather is given by "the world's wide mouth." At Hotspur's death the meaning of "name" changes through chiming repetitions from the earlier "proper name" to the newly current "repute":

> *Hotspur.* If I mistake not, thou art Harry Monmouth.
> *Prince.* Thou speak'st as if I would deny my name.
> *Hot.* My name is Harry Percy.
> *Prince.* Why then I see
>   A very valiant rebel of the name.
> · · · · · · · · · · · · · · · · ·
> *Hot.* . . . and would to God
> Thy name in arms were now as great as mine!
> ·
> *Hot.* . . . I better brook the loss of brittle life
> Than those proud titles thou has won of me.
>   (V.iv.58–78)

In comparison to the controlling conception of name in *R2*, the idea of name as repute in *1H4* is notably secular and takes into account the fact that name is a social phenomenon. Thus in *1H4* we have a midpoint between two extremes: (1) Richard's idea of name as a sacred absolute unaffected by usage, and (2) the idea expressed in *2H4* by Doll Tearsheet:

> A Captain? God's light, these villains will make the word as odious as the word 'occupy,' which was an excellent good word before it was ill sorted: therefore captains had need look to't
>   (*2H4*, II.iv.143–47)

in which not merely names but all words are taken to be not merely social phenomena but, further, entirely subject to perversion by usage.

"Name," thus, provides an index of how operative conceptions of language in *1H4* differ from those in *R2*. But a further index of the change is that "name" in *1H4* is no longer of such central importance as in *R2*; so that it provides a kind of *R2*-based perspective, one which we may now abandon to consider briefly some other ways in which language is conceived in *1H4*.

Although, as I have said, calling as summoning rather than as dubbing is prominent in

> *Glendower.* I can call spirits from the vasty deep.
> *Hotspur.* Why, so can I, or so can any man, But will
> they come when you do call for them?
>   (III.i.50–52)

the wit of Hotspur's reply has nothing to do with the two kinds of calling, or even with summoning as a specific kind of illocutionary act, but rather with the difference between what Austin terms illocutionary and perlocutionary acts. Austin, it will be remembered, uses urging as an example of an illocutionary act (one done *in* speech), and persuading as an example of a corresponding perlocutionary act (done *through* speech)— "corresponding" because in urging one does or tries to persuade.[5] Hotspur's witty misinterpretation of Glendower's meaning depends on the fact that "call," as it happens, can mean either an illocution ("to summon"), as Hotspur takes it, or a perlocution ("to make to come"), as Glendower means it.

Hotspur's joke—which Austin, one imagines, must have appreciated—is symptomatic of the fact that generally in *1H4* references to language involve the conceiving of language as the instrument or medium of acts done in and through speech, along the speaker-hearer axis. If "Renaissance" means "practical," this is obviously a Renaissance way of conceiving of language, and it distinguishes *1H4* from *R2*, where these matters are obscured by the reigning conception of language. The difference between the two plays is the difference between the crisp clarity of Hotspur's playing with the illocution-perlocution distinction and Richard's

> We were not born to sue but to command;
> Which since we cannot do to make you friends
>   (*R2*. I.i.196–97)

in which he muddles the same distinction. In *1H4*, within a context of kinds of speech acts involving essential conceptual reference to action, the idea of speech itself as a kind of action is a natural basis for play such as Hotspur's, or Falstaff's

[5]See above, Chapter 2.

> I deny your major. If you will deny the sheriff, so . . .
> (II.iv.489)

playing on "deny" as a verbal and a nonverbal act.

This play of Falstaff's embodies another way of attending to language, one which becomes newly important in the play. To "deny" is one of a large group of references to language which concern the truth and falsity of propositions. In *1H4* the true or false propositions are generally descriptions of external factual reality that exist in a realm of social intercourse where their accuracy can be challenged and tested (unlike the proposition involved in Richard's attempt to express "the truth of what I am"). This way of conceiving of language centers to a large extent around Falstaff (false staff), who, according to Hal, is the father of lies (II.iv.220). It is a conception of language which in the beginning of the tetralogy was ruled out by Richard's obfuscation of the factual truth of Woodstock's death. Now, after Richard's fall, it surfaces again. In *2H4* it continues to be important, though there the optimism about the value of scientific-historical description wanes; in *H5* it subsides again— not, as in *R2*, through being proscribed, but rather through being transcended.

In such ways, then, references to speech and language in *1H4* manifest ways of conceiving of and attending to the subject that distinguish this play from *R2*. The qualitative change is also apparent in the ways language is used—in the verbal action. I have already touched on some of the newly important features of speech action in *1H4*; I want now to consider more intensively one such feature, that of "control," which seems to typify the distinctive speech action of the play.

II

In many interchanges it is possible to establish that one of the parties is controlling the conversation. There may or may not be apparent reasons for his control, and the reasons may be of various kinds (the speaker's office, his "strength of character," etc.). But within the speech action itself there are fairly definite and constant manifestations of control. In Henry's "private conference" with Hal (III.ii; discussed below, pp. 80–83), the king's imperatives are his most obvious bids for control. Any imperative may be a bid for control, of course; but Henry's have particularly to do with control *within speech action* because they are in fact commands to speak, which Hal finally obeys satisfactorily. Furthermore, Henry's control and Hal's obedience are manifested by the fact that it is always Henry, and never Hal, who introduces a topic of conversation.[6]

Now this kind of control of speech interaction is very little at issue in *R2*, where Richard's absolutism so little admits interaction that silence seems the best tactic of opposition. But when at his fall real interaction becomes more possible, the question of control in that interaction becomes more important. This is fairly obvious in scenes like the long interchange between Henry and Hal, and even more in Henry's scene with Hotspur. But I would argue that the feature of control is also significant in scenes in which the general questions of authority and obedience are far less obviously at issue. Indeed, throughout *1H4* this feature is more significant—is, as it were, more an object of the dramaturgy—than in *R2*. Its general importance is established in the first two scenes, in which it operates in sharply contrasting fashions.

In the first brief scene with Henry, Lancaster, Westmoreland, Blunt, and others, we have a decorously ordered court in which there is genuine interaction controlled entirely by the king. Henry speaks at times to everyone present (the first vocative is his "friends," l. 18) but only Westmoreland replies, so that the scene amounts to a kind of dialogue in which the control is most obviously manifest in the transitions from one speaker to the other.

Henry initiates the action, first addressing all present and then concluding his speech with an address to Westmoreland:

> Then let me hear
> Of you, my gentle cousin Westmoreland,

[6]The study of "turn-taking" in ordinary conversation has recently become a special field of sociolinguistic study. For one of the most accessible results, with a fairly detailed bibliography, see Starkey Duncan, Jr., "Some Signals and Rules for Taking Speaking Turns in Conversations." Duncan is concerned primarily with cues for turn-taking involving nonverbal communication, unlike those treated here.

What yesternight our Council did decree
In forwarding this dear expedience.
(I.i.30–33)

The change of address in mid-speech is an assertion of authority—Henry will address whom he pleases—and the concluding
command or request to Westmoreland is a bid for control of the
interaction. Westmoreland accepts the bid, replying as re-
quested about the appointed subject. He shows some initiative
in introducing, in this speech and his next, the "heavy news" of
fighting in Wales and the North; even so, he frames these
speeches so that his introduction of the news "counts as" an
answer to Henry's question. The end of his speech is simply
that—he has finished obeying Henry's command to speak, and
he makes no bid for control.

The entire scene consists of ten such movements. In each
case,[7] moving from a speech of Henry's to one of Westmoreland's, we see the latter obeying the former's command to
speak. Sometimes, as above, the command is explicit, sometimes not, as in the next interchange,

> *King.* It seems then that the tidings of this broil
> Brake off our business for the Holy Land.
> *West.* This matched with other did, my gracious lord,
> (ll. 47–49)

in which Westmoreland obeys some such implicit command as
"Verify the hypothesis I state." But the command is always there
and is always obeyed. Moving from one of Westmoreland's
speeches to one of Henry's we always find Westmoreland simply concluding without any bid for control and then Henry taking the initiative to further the action. When, within a speech,
Westmoreland introduces a topic he always, as above, shows
the relevance of the newer topic to that under discussion so that
he never presumes to "change the subject." Henry, however,
introduces new subjects freely.

All this is to say that the direction of control of the interaction
is constant and unchallenged throughout the scene. The situation of Henry's court is rather like that of those model children

[7]With possibly one unimportant exception: Westmoreland's "I will, my
liege" (I.i.107).

who speak when spoken to. Inasmuch as they *are* spoken to,
they are generally more fortunate than was Richard's court.

The next scene gives us a very different state of affairs, right
from the opening interchange:

> *Falstaff.* Now, Hal, what time of day is it, lad?
> *Prince.* Thou art so fat-witted with drinking of old sack,
> and unbuttoning thee after supper, and sleeping
> upon benches after noon, that thou hast forgotten to
> demand that truly which thou wouldst truly know.
> What a devil hast thou to do with the time of the
> day? Unless hours were cups of sack, and minutes
> capons, and clocks the tongues of bawds, and dials
> the signs of leaping-houses, and the blessed sun
> himself a fair hot wench in flame-coloured taffeta, I
> see no reason why thou shouldst be so superfluous
> to demand the time of the day.
>
> (I.ii.1–12)

The content of this interchange shows Falstaff as oblivious to the
fact of the passage of time, a characteristic of him subsequently
apparent in numerous ways, whereas Hal in his mocking shows
himself to be of a different mind.[8] But what is of immediate
concern to us is the operation of the feature of control here.
Falstaff initiates the action with a question. This constitutes a bid
for control because a question is a special kind of imperative; a
request or command or, as Hal here calls it, a "demand," to
speak to the specified topic.[9] Hal, however, does not obey; he
does not answer the question—initially he does not even handle
the specified topic. Instead of obeying, he plays upon Falstaff's
question, twice referring to its status as "demand," and himself
bids for control by a ("rhetorical") question of his own, and by

---

[8]And see below, p. 79

[9]The "interrogative" and "imperative" moods seem to be alternative realizations in the surface grammar of a single feature of the deep grammar, a deep-grammar imperative. The "interrogative" mood generally is used when the action imperated is verbal, the "imperative" when it is not. But even these surface distinctions are not absolute. An interrogative ("Who are you?") is generally replaceable by an imperative ("Tell me who you are"). And in certain situations we replace an imperative for nonverbal action ("Pass the salt") with an interrogative ("Will you pass the salt?"). I owe the salt example to Julian Boyd and James Peter Thorne, "The Deep Grammar of Model Verbs," *ERIC/PEGS* 31 (16 April 1968).

introducing new topics of conversation. As far as control is concerned, then, there obtains something of a draw at this point.

Falstaff could now entirely accept Hal's bids for control by answering the question directly and speaking to the topics Hal has introduced, or he could entirely decline by doing neither. His procedure is in fact something between the two, and very characteristic, as he says

> Indeed, you come near me now, Hal, for we that take
> purses go by the moon and the seven stars, and not
> "by Phoebus, he, that wand'ring knight so fair": and I
> prithee sweet wag, when thou art king, as God save
> thy Grace—Majesty I should say, for grace thou wilt
> have none.
>
> (ll. 13–18)

For, while ostensibly beginning to answer—to obey Hal's "demand"—he changes the subject by taking Hal's "day" other than as it was meant.[10]

Hal's following

> What, none?
>
> (l. 19)

is perhaps the strongest assertion of authority or bid for control in the interaction thus far, because it is a question almost *tout court* and also an interruption of the speech of his interlocutor.

When Falstaff replies

> No, by my troth, not so much as will serve to be
> prologue to an egg and butter
>
> (ll. 20–21)

he largely accepts this bid for control—he in no way resists or challenges Hal's right to interrupt him and, instead of refusing to answer the question (as Hal has done three speeches before), he obeys the "demand." Hal's

> Well, how then? Come, roundly, roundly.
>
> (l. 22)

[10]That is to say, he "judgeth false" as at I.ii.63 and often thereafter. Humphreys in his note on ii.4–7 describes Falstaff's wilful misinterpretation of Hal's "day."

directs Falstaff to finish his sentence, and his prompt obedience further establishes that Hal now controls the interaction.

Through the next three speeches, until Falstaff's final question, we have neutral ground as far as control is concerned, inasmuch as there are no questions, interruptions, or abrupt changes of subject:

> *Fal.* Marry then sweet wag, when thou art king let not us that are squires of the night's body be called thieves of the day's beauty: let us be Diana's foresters, gentlemen of the shade, minions of the moon; and let men say we be men of good government, being governed as the sea is, by our noble and chaste mistress the moon, under whose countenance we steal.
>
> *Prince.* Thou sayest well, and it holds well too, for the fortune of us that are the moon's men doth ebb and flow like the sea, being governed as the sea is, by the moon—as for proof now, a purse of gold most resolutely snatched on Monday night, and most dissolutely spent on Tuesday morning, got with swearing "Lay by!", and spent with crying "Bring in!", now in as low an ebb as the foot of the ladder, and by and by in as high a flow as the ridge of the gallows.
>
> *Fal.* By the Lord thou say'st true, lad; and is not my hostess of the tavern a most sweet wench?
>
> (ll. 23–40)

But the question of control of verbal action is raised, tangentially at least, when Falstaff completes a polite ("I prithee") and play-ful ("sweet wag") bid for regulation of the speech of the nation ("let not us . . . be called . . . and let men say. . . ."). The nor-mal reaction to such an imperative for future action is recogni-tion of the imperative in a promise or a refusal to do what is demanded; and this holds true whether or not the converse is playful. But Hal, playing with the figure of the "moon's men," simply ignores Falstaff's request. Also in this interchange, in the chiming comments

> *Prince.* Thou sayest well

and

Fal. . . . thou say'st true,

what will prove to be part of an important distinction between
their uses of language is lightly touched on.

In any case, Falstaff, who has temporarily accepted Hal's control of the interaction, now makes another bid for control with
his concluding "demand." This time Hal accedes by answering,
but immediately makes a demand of his own:

> As the honey of Hybla, my old lad of the castle; and is
> not a buff jerkin a most sweet robe of durance?
> (ll. 41–42)

And now, as though encouraged by Hal's having accepted his
bid for control, Falstaff refuses for the first time to accept a bid of
the prince's—

> How now, how now, mad wag? What, in thy quips
> and quiddities? What a plague have I to do with a buff
> jerkin?
> (ll. 43–45)

—countering one demand with another. Interestingly this, his
most aggressive maneuver thus far in the interchange, is a copy
or echo from Hal's "What a devil hast thou to do with the time of
day?" showing Falstaff with the power quickly to learn and
employ Hal's own maneuvers against him; and perhaps there
is the hint of a certain poverty of invention in so rapid and
mechanical an imitation.

Hal seems to imply something like "If merely repeating maneuvers is what you want, let's do that: I see your game" when he
uses the same form again, to refuse Falstaff's demand and to
make one of his own:

> Why, what a pox have I to do with my hostess of the
> tavern?
> (ll. 46–47)

Now Falstaff again accepts Hal's control of the interaction by
answering, that is, by obeying his "demand." The prince immediately presses with another demand, as if to emphasize his
control of the action, and Falstaff, again submits:

> *Fal.* Well, thou hast called her to a reckoning many a
> time and oft.

> *Prince.* Did I ever call for thee to pay thy part?
> *Fal.* No, I'll give thee thy due, thou hast paid all there.
>
> (ll. 48–51)

And so it goes. The last speeches quoted comprise a minor climax; subsequently in the scene more of the interaction is neutral in terms of control, and where control is at issue it generally rests with Hal. Yet Falstaff continues to make occasional bids for control and to refuse those of Hal.

In interaction like that between Henry and Westmoreland where from speech to speech there is no change in the configuration of the variables that constitute control, we can give a simple description of the action as a whole in terms of control—for example, the first scene is controlled by Henry. But in the scene with Hal and Falstaff we find, moving from speech to speech, virtually every possible configuration of these variables so that, while at any point we can give a local description in terms of control, such a description of the entire action cannot be simple. Still, in the interchange taken as a whole, the play of control does have a design whose significance we apprehend much as we apprehend the significance of musical patterns. In this interaction, for instance, the state of complete and unchallenged control by Hal is like the tonic key with reference to which we order the movement, and to which we know it must return. This is not because most of the action transpires in that state—it does not—but rather because of the context in which it occurs. For example, in the interchanges discussed it is significant that the configuration of control variables shifts, never being quite the same from speech to speech, until Falstaff refuses to obey Hal's "demand." He makes a "demand" of his own, thus moving farther than before from the "tonic," at which point the action modulates immediately into the "tonic," with the control variables remaining constant now through several speeches. So it is that the first scene with Hal and Falstaff establishes a kind of key for the entirety of their interaction.

And this sort of control is significant not only in the first two scenes of *1H4* but also through the rest of the "justling time" (IV.i.18) of the play, where it continues to be an important dimension of the linguistic realm in which the four major characters, to whom we now turn, exist and define themselves.

III

Of these four characters, Hotspur is the most isolated: his rebellion sets him against the other three so that he has comparatively little interaction with them. Furthermore, he seems more static than the others because in his first scene he is characterized very fully and subsequently we find out little more about his character. Therefore it seems appropriate to restrict our attention primarily to the scene (I.iii) of Hotspur's confrontation with Henry followed by his talk with the men of his party, Worcester and Northumberland.

In Hotspur's first speech—consisting mostly of his vigorous and amusing description of the lord "perfumed like a milliner" sent by Henry to demand the prisoners—much of his scorn is directed at the man's "holiday and lady terms" and his "bald unjointed chat." This, in keeping with Hotspur's later amusement at his wife's genteel oaths and his scorn of poetry, seems to exemplify a peremptoriness and impatience with certain *manners* of speech, an impatience that also perhaps appears in his "speaking thick" and, more generally, an interest in those very manners, in the "terms," perhaps at the expense of attention to the nature of the act itself.

Here this distribution of attention is a diversionary tactic: focusing on the "terms" and manner of the man's speech, Hotspur glosses over the action itself, the man's demand and his own reply:

> With many holiday and lady terms
> He question'd me, amongst the rest demanded
> My prisoners in your Majesty's behalf.
> I then . . .
> Answer'd neglectingly, I know not what,
> He should, or he should not . . .
> I answer'd indirectly, as I said.
> 　　　　　　　　　(I.iii.45–65)

Furthermore, Hotspur's ridicule of the manner of the man's speech may be in the interest of lending support to the plea with which he ends the speech:

> And I beseech you, let not his report
> Come current for an accusation

Betwixt my love and your high Majesty.
(I.iii.66–68)

In other words, "His report is as ridiculous as the *manner* in which it must have been given to you."

Yet we do not, I think, feel Hotspur's tactic here as quite calculated; rather we take it that he really is at this moment, unlikely as it seems, unable to recall what he said to the lord, though he remembers in such detail what the lord said to him.

In his next speech Hotspur again seizes on "terms," but here the matter is more serious:

> *Henry.* . . . I shall never hold that man my friend
>   Whose tongue shall ask me for one penny cost
>   To ransom home revolted Mortimer.
> *Hotspur.* Revolted Mortimer!
>   He never did fall off, my sovereign liege,
>   But by the chance of war. . . .
>   . . . .
>   Then let him not be slander'd with revolt.
>   (I.iii.89–111)

The passionate conviction behind the daring and even foolhardiness of Hotspur's so accusing his "sovereign liege" of slander is perhaps even more strikingly manifest in the second sentence of

> He never did fall off, my sovereign,
>   But by the chance of war: to prove that true
>   Needs no more but one tongue for all those wounds
>   . . . which valiantly he took.
>   (I.iii.93–96)

The "one tongue" is Hotspur's own. His confidence in it is the obverse of his scorn of the perfumed lord's tongue. But Hotspur's "proof" is no more than a report, like that of the lord's. It is merely a counterclaim to Henry's claim, and it is only in Hotspur's mind that his "one tongue" sweeps kings like perfumed lords before it.

His peremptoriness rouses Henry to forbid him to speak of Mortimer, and this especially angers Hotspur:

> Speak of Mortimer?
> 'Zounds, I will speak of him.
>   (I.iii.128–29)

In the remainder of the scene, as he talks with Worcester and Northumberland, his anger and passionate conviction are displayed in extravagant boasts and threats. Northumberland justly complains of his "Tying thine ear to no tongue but thine own," and Worcester that "You start away; / And lend no ear unto my purposes." Refusing to listen to his compeers, Hotspur impatiently interrupts to speak his own mind, and threatens to monopolize the conversation. At one point, when he has spoken for twenty-eight lines and is continuing "Therefore, I say—" Worcester interrupts with "Peace, cousin, say no more." While Hotspur's "one tongue" is vigorous and often startlingly beautiful, as in his "methinks it were an easy leap, / To pluck bright honour from the pale-fac'd moon," Worcester's comment on this speech is telling: "He apprehends a world of figures here, / But not the form of what he should attend."

This comment of Worcester's seems especially to indicate the way in which Hotspur's speech action is fundamentally like that of Richard II. For all the differences in temperament and imagination, Hotspur is another Richard in tying his ear to his own one tongue and its world of figures, in not attending and giving audience to the world of people around him.

But the Renaissance noble does not have the guaranteed audience of the medieval king. Whereas Richard's audience abetted the hypertrophy of *his* "one tongue," Hotspur must chafe against King Henry's refusal to hear *his*:

> He said he would not ransom Mortimer,
> Forbad my tongue to speak of Mortimer,
> But I will find him when he lies asleep,
> And in his ear I'll holla "Mortimer!"
> Nay, I'll have a starling shall be taught to speak
> Nothing but "Mortimer," and give it him
> To keep his anger still in motion.
>
> (I.iii.217–23)

This seems like essential Hotspur in its engaging extravagance, in the fact that it follows directly on the heels of a serious vow ("Nay, I will keep the prisoners: that's flat!"), and also for the particular content, the "figure" involved. It is right that Hotspur should think of the starling and of substituting it for himself, because the talking bird is in a sense the extreme toward which he tends in his unconscious impulsive noncommunicative speaking.[11]

His next scene (II.iii) gives us two further striking examples of Hotspur as starling or, as his wife calls him there, "paraquito" (l. 86). He enters *"solus, reading a letter"* from a fickle nobleman, aloud, and interrupting his reading to indulge in impulsive addresses to the writer of the letter:

> . . . but I tell you, my lord fool, out of this nettle,
> danger, we pluck this flower, safety
> (II.iii.9–10)

and

> Say you so, say you so? I say unto you again, you are a
> shallow cowardly hind, and you lie.
> (II.iii.14–16)

[11]The association of Hotspur with talking birds is strengthened by the fact that his wife later calls him a "paraquito" (II.iii.86) and also, ironically, that he himself calls the perfumed lord a "popinjay," or parrot (I.iii.49). That Hotspur is a kind of talking bird also explains a passage which has troubled commentators, the speech in which Hal speaks first of Francis ("Anon, anon, sir") and then of Hotspur:

> That ever this fellow should have fewer words than a parrot, and yet
> the son of a woman! His industry is up-stairs and down-stairs, his
> eloquence the parcel of a reckoning. I am not yet of Percy's mind, the
> Hotspur of the north, he that kills me some six or seven dozen of Scots
> at a breakfast.
> (II.iv.96–101)

In his note on the passage Humphreys says

> This change of subject is surprising. The connection may lie, as
> Johnson suggested, in Hal's contrasting his "all humours" with
> Hotspur's homicidal monomania; or in Francis's busy-ness, or his limi-
> tation of ideas; or in all of these. This is Hal's first reference to Hotspur
> and he instinctively recognizes the antithesis between his own so-
> ciable nature and his rival's combative militarism.

This seems generally true, but the change of subject turns on the word "parrot," and the specific immediate connection that leads from Francis to Hotspur is the *similarity in their use of language.* J. D. Schuchter, in "Prince Hal and Francis," also missing the associative link, remarks lamely that

> The Arden editor says that the "change of subject is surprising"
> . . . but it is only the kind of shifting, sorting and comparing that Hal
> does all the time. All that is ellipsed is *"I am not like Francis, but on the
> other* hand I am not yet of Percy's mind."

In *2H4* there is an echo of this train of association when, in a scene with Francis, in which Hal and Poins imitate his "anon, anon, sir" (II.iv.279), Hal speaks of Falstaff as being "like a parrot" (257).

The lord, of course, is not there to reply; and Hotspur seems in his element in this energetic noncommunication. Then, later in the scene, in Lady Percy's long and impressive description of Hotspur's talking in his sleep (ll. 48–63), we have him engaging in speech which is quite literally unconscious, impulsive, and noncommunicative.

Thus, in Hotspur's first appearances there is a great deal of emphasis on the special nature of his language. Or, to put the matter differently, much of the striking characterization is in terms of peculiarly limited ways of conceiving of and using language. Throughout the remainder of the play his fortunes rise and fall, but his linguistic world seems not to change until death lays its "cold and earthy hand" (V.iv.83) on his tongue, interrupting him, just as his fellows have had to do, in mid-sentence.

IV

Falstaff's most famous remark about language is probably

> What is honour? A word. What is in that word honour? What is that honour? Air.
>
> (V.i.134–35)

The remark is interesting as a kind of pendant to the development we have observed in Richard's thought about name: the first part of Falstaff's remark is a direct expression of the nominalism Richard approached at his fall. The problem of the status of the essence or universal "king" had driven Richard toward the idea that no nomenclature is adequate, in other words, to doubt the efficacy of any nomenclature to attribute essences or universals and thence (by implication, at least) to skepticism about the universals themselves. But Falstaff goes beyond such skepticism when he denies that there is a universal or essence corresponding to the word "honor"—claiming that the word names nothing, that there is no honor, but only "honor." Nor is Falstaff here at all despairing, as Richard was when he approached such extremes. Rather he seems blithely assured.

Thus Falstaff the nominalist, scoffing at "quips and . . . quiddities" (I.ii.43–44), is the peculiar terminus of much of

Richard's speculation about language. The problem, of course, is that Falstaff's nominalism is as naively assumed as Richard's initial realism, and, in its way, is as mistakenly absolutist. Falstaff has given a different answer to the same sort of question that troubled Richard; and the question itself indicated a way of conceiving of language that the tetralogy moves beyond— though there is a kind of final victory for realism when Richard's "name of king," descending on Falstaff's boon companion, turns out not quite simply to be "A word."

But there is more than nominalism in Falstaff's remark about honor. It is reductive, which nominalism need not be. This is partly because the remark also expresses a peculiarly gross and extreme kind of materialism. Now materialism and its concurrent reductiveness are evident in much of Falstaff's behavior. But what makes this instance interesting and surprising is the application of the materialism to language—surely a grotesque misapplication. The materialism involved in Falstaff's concern for his body may be a tonic antidote to Hotspur's chivalric heedless idealism. But the materialism of "What is in that word honour? . . . Air" is toxic even though it may look like an antidote to Hotspur's absorption in his "world of figures"; for it ignores everything essential. It is difficult to imagine bodiless chivalry, but we do not even have to imagine verbal communication that does not depend on air for transmission—we have the written word as an example. Thus Falstaff in making this remark is doing more than exhaling and so in a manner refuting himself.[12]

It may seem that I take Falstaff's remark more seriously and literally than it deserves since, even though this is soliloquy, there is a large element of playful wit involved. However, I would argue that in the first place there is *always* a large element of playful wit in what Falstaff says, and in the second place that the remark expresses, however lightly, something importantly characteristic, that Falstaff generally practices what he preaches here about language.

If what words contain is "air," in a sense one can do anything one wants with them. And such an implication is involved in a number of ways in Falstaff's speech action. Most obviously,

---

[12]I think that this paradox is less idle than it may appear. Self-refutation seems typical of Falstaff—as with his claiming to be young, or his patent lies.

perhaps, he treats words as "air" in the linguistic playfulness of his figures, comparisons, and puns. More importantly, he acts as though he can do as he likes with words in the ways he overrides the social dimension of speech acts. Irresponsible in reporting, in making promises, and the like, unconstrained by obligations to truth or to keeping his word, Falstaff is on a year-long holiday from what Searle has called the "institutional facts" of language. And his holiday irresponsibility is apparent not only in his own speech acts but also in the way he takes the speech acts of others, as when he does not heed Hal's, and later the Lord Chief Justice's, warnings.

One of the most interesting and distinctive manifestations of this attitude is Falstaff's soliloquies. They differ from those of Richard, Henry, and Hal, and indeed from those of almost all Shakespeare's other characters, inasmuch as Falstaff does not reveal or give himself away to us in them much more than he gives himself away to other characters of the drama in speech actually directed at them. He is as playfully evasive and irresponsible with us or himself—whichever we take his soliloquies as being directed toward—as he is with his interlocutors. This makes him enigmatic and fascinating, to be sure. But it seems also important for exemplifying a kind of rigidity inherent in his excessive freedom from responsibility. And it further establishes that while he has no quite public self, role, or character—not really being involved in affairs of the realm—neither does he have the quite private self usually exhibited in soliloquy.

In some respects, Falstaff's use of language is like Hotspur's. What Worcester says of Hotspur's speech, for instance, could also apply to much of Falstaff's: "He apprehends a world of figures here, / But not the form of what he should attend." But in *1H4* the differences between Hotspur's impulsive, impatient rhetoric and Falstaff's airy wordplay are more notable than the similarities. And the inherent problems and limitations of Falstaff's language, being subtler, take longer—in the tetralogy and in this study—to deal with.

V

While Hal's speech about the "leash of drawers" (discussed above) exhibits ways in which the conceptual linguistic "world" of 1H4 differs from that of R2, it also of course exhibits Hal's own characteristic ways of thinking about language. What seems most important there is that he shows himself to be conscious of the variety of tongues and as having learned a new one, that is, as a kind of polyglot. This characterization of him becomes increasingly explicit and significant as the tetralogy progresses, but already in 1H4 its applicability is apparent. Facility with the very different languages of tavern and court is perhaps the most obvious mark of his proficiency. There is also the fact that his speech ranges all the way from his entirely private soliloquy in I.ii to his entirely public and official (his first such speech act) determination that the prisoner Douglas is to be freed (V.v.25–31).

This interest in variety of languages and polyglotism seems the most important general characteristic of Hal's way of thinking about language, showing him as asking questions about language which are fundamentally different from those asked by Richard (and Falstaff). The realist-nominalist inquiry into the essential nature of language itself, centering on the question of name, having proved a futile obsession with Richard, having subsided to occasional echoes in Henry and Falstaff, to Hal seems of no concern. Rather, we see him beginning playfully to handle problems of translation and thus, more than anyone else in the play, to attend to and accept the situation which has in a sense resulted from and in a sense caused Richard's fall: the fact of the variety of languages.

One other pronounced characteristic of Hal's language deserves particular note. While his linguistic flexibility is manifest in his performing and mentioning a considerable variety of kinds of speech act, there is one which he mentions and performs frequently, distinctively, and emphatically enough for it to be considered typical of him. This is the group of *promising* and other similar speech acts such as vowing, swearing, and giving one's word.

Promises are, so to speak, in the air in 1H4, distinguishing the linguistic world there from that of R2, and not all of them directly concern Hal; but his promises seem to constitute the example for interpreting and judging the others. In Act III, scene ii, we have a good instance of this. The climax of the scene (and a major turning point of the play) is the most explicit and solemn promise in *1H4*, Hal's "this vow" (l. 159), which "in the name of God I promise here" (l. 153) to "redeem all this on Percy's head" (l. 132.). Almost immediately after Hal's solemn promise to his father, Blunt enters to announce that there is to be a battle at Shrewsbury, saying of the rebels that

> A mighty and a fearful head they are,
> If promises be kept on every hand.
> (III.ii.167–68)

This points to more than the simple dramatic irony of our knowledge that the rebels do not keep their promises to each other. For clearly we are meant to compare their promising with Hal's to his father and, further, to realize that if promises *are* kept on every hand, that is, if Hal's to his father is kept, the rebels must lose, however mighty and fearful they might be. This is an especially clear example, but I think it is true generally that the play's promises are to be appreciated with reference to Hal.[13]

Regarding Hal thus as a central promiser involves taking into account, as far as possible, all his promising and certainly his explicit references to the act of promising. In particular it involves attending to his

> So when this loose behaviour I throw off,
> And pay the debt I never promised,
> By how much better than my word I am,
> By so much shall I falsify men's hopes.
> (I.ii.203–6)

This occurs in his famous, or notorious, soliloquy at the end of his first scene, a speech which has often figured in the critical controversy about his character. It is favorite evidence of hypocrisy and mean conniving for those who find these qualities in Hal, and has been something of a thorn in the flesh of those who do not. Although my concerns and approach differ from the traditional ones in that controversy, I think that the troublesome

---

[13]Professor John Anson points out that the emphasis in *1H4* on degrees and ways of keeping promises "looks forward to the crucial prevarication in Part Two at Gaultree."

aspect of the speech can be brought into sharper focus by the notion of speech act.

Samuel Johnson's comment is representative of a certain critical fuzziness which has persisted:

> This speech is very artfully introduced to keep the prince from appearing vile in the opinion of the audience: it prepares them for his future reformation, and, what is yet more valuable, exhibits a natural picture of a great mind offering excuses to itself, and palliating those follies which it can neither justify nor forsake.[14]

It seems odd, in the first place, that Johnson is telling us *what the speech does*, rather than what *Hal* is doing—the latter is more directly relevant to a moral judgment of the character.

What Hal is doing is, in fact, strange and difficult to define. In the four lines quoted above, the characteristic seriousness and scrupulousness about promising and keeping one's word pose no problem; but there is a problem in that the disclaimer of promising is part of an apparent promise—indeed the whole soliloquy looks like a kind of promise.

But if the speech is a promise, it is fundamentally different from what Johnson's representative comment seems to imply. To Johnson it seems that the speech is a report, with excuses and palliations, of a state of mind, so that the parts of the speech referring to future actions are not promises but statements of intention.

This ambiguity can arise because, since the act is not explicit (i.e., Hal says neither "I hereby promise" nor "I hereby state my intentions"), we must infer the illocutionary force. That the question is important for a moral assessment of Hal can be seen, I think, if we consider rough translations which are unambiguously

> (A) *statement of intent:* "My intention is to throw off this loose behavior, falsify men's hopes, etc."

[14]*The Plays of William Shakespeare,* ed. Samuel Johnson, 8 vols. (London, 1765), quoted by Humphreys in his note on the passage.

and

> (B) *promise:* "I promise to throw off this loose behavior, falsify men's hopes, etc."

With (A) Hal is autonomous—he has a plan which he deigns to state; and this fits with the picture of him as a sort of hypocritical schemer. With (B), however, Hal is placing himself under an obligation to act in a certain way—he is being morally responsible. Thus it is important to decide of what sort Hal's illocutionary act is.

The decision is made easier by considering direction of address. The speech begins—

> I know you all, and will awhile uphold
> The unyok'd humour of your idleness

—so that the first possibility to be considered is that it is entirely an apostrophe, explicitly directed to "you all": Poins, Falstaff, and company.[15] This is incorrect, however, because (1) Shakespeare is usually careful about marking the extent of apostrophe by repeatedly making the direction of address explicit throughout, while here, after the first sentence, there are no more markers for an apostrophe to "you all"; and (2) Falstaff, Poins, and company must be included in the "men" whose hopes Hal is going to falsify by redeeming time when they least expect it, implying that he is no longer addressing them—otherwise he would be using a second, not a third, person.

It seems therefore that the direction of address must change after the first sentence, and that we must take the remainder of the speech as being addressed to himself, to the play's audience, or to an unnamed, vague, and general third hearer such as God. This, in the first place, removes the apparent contradiction of his promising to pay a debt he never undertook: he can be promis-

---

[15]In the production of the tetralogy at Stratford in 1951, the first two lines of the soliloquy—

> I know you all, and will awhile uphold
> The unyok'd humour of your idleness

—seem to have been addressed to the audience, which must have been very odd indeed (v. J. Dover Wilson and T. C. Worsley, *Shakespeare's Histories at Stratford, 1951*, p. 47).

ing to the present addressee what he never vowed to "men."
With that difficulty removed, Hal's references to keeping one's
word and promising could support our regarding the speech
itself as a promise. As the only references to illocutionary action
in the speech these direct our attention toward promising, give
us that mental set, and show the one specific kind of speech act
that occupies Hal's mind.

If we further consider direction of address, the speech taken
as (A), a declaration of state of mind including intent and addressed to a general unnamed hearer such as God, seems rather
pointless, this sort of hearer presumably being omniscient; but
as (B), a promise, the speech makes sense so addressed—God is
just the sort of hearer to whom people (including Hal later in his
career) make promises. If we take the speech as addressed to
himself, (B) continues to be more probable. Although a declaration to oneself of the state of one's mind is conceivable, it would
seem normally to occur only at the moment of discovering or
understanding that state of mind—as with Richard's final soliloquy. And in fact, Hal's speech does not give the impression
that he is discovering or understanding a state of mind as he
enunciates it to himself. On the other hand, there is nothing strange about making a vow or promise (a "resolution") to
oneself.

If we take the speech as being directed to the play's audience,
the balance might seem to rest either way, but such an address
seems far less likely than the other two. The matter is complicated by the dramatic irony of the audience's knowledge that
Hall *will* reform. There would be some justification for his stating his intention to reform inasmuch as the audience does not
know that at this point in his career he already has that intention. There would also be justification of his promising the play's
audience to reform, since their foreknowledge does in a sense
constitute an obligation for him. However, this direction of address still seems less likely than the other two because Hal does
not elsewhere seem to take the play's audience into account.

Thus a consideration of the illocutionary force and direction
of address of Hal's famous soliloquy supports its being understood as a promise directed to himself or to an unnamed hearer
such as God, and thus it provides evidence for a moral assess-

ment of him, evidence that apparently makes it impossible to regard him as a scheming hypocrite.¹⁶

As far as the tetralogy as a developing whole is concerned, Hal's characteristic promising is important as it contrasts him with Richard. Richard's last major speech is the soliloquy in which, realizing that "I wasted time, and now doth time waste me," he plays desperately and nervously with figures of clocks, dials, minutes, and hours (*R2*, V.v.1–66). In Hal's first speech he plays with the same figures, not nervously but with easy assurance. What the echo suggests proves true: attitude toward time is a criterion for establishing important differences between the two men, and these differences inform their respective conceptions and uses of language. As I have tried to show, Richard's absolutist conception of language excludes the fact of the passage of time; and his characteristic speech acts, such as defining, equating, naming, do not involve essential conceptual reference to time. But Hal from the beginning takes time very much into account—thinks of himself as existing in time. And his characteristic promising itself involves such reference to the fact of time's passage, from the present moment of the promise to the future moment of its fulfillment.

VI

There are good reasons for Henry's relative neglect by audiences and critics. If Hotspur is most isolated from interaction with the other major characters, it is Henry of these other four who is most isolated from the action in general. His court seems underpopulated in comparison with the rebel camp, and it is the locale of a comparatively small part of the play's action. Furthermore, Henry seems less remarkable than the other three—less engaging than Hotspur, less fascinating than Falstaff and, perhaps even here, less formidable than Hal. Nevertheless, he does, I think, deserve more attention than he has usually received.

¹⁶In the controversy about Hal's moral character not enough attention has been paid to his offer to engage in single combat with Hotspur at Shrewsbury "to save the blood on either side" (V.v.99). This, apparently Shakespeare's invention, suggests at least his intentions about Hal's character.

Henry's position is more difficult than that of any other major character in the tetralogy; therefore, in a sense, he can afford none of the extravagances that make Richard, Falstaff, Hotspur, and Hal interesting. He is, for instance, quite humorless, yet not pompous; and that combination in itself is fairly exceptional in Shakespeare. The limitations of his speech action are generally, to a striking degree, those of his directness, economy, and authoritative forthrightness.[17] That these qualities have become somewhat blurred in the criticism may be partly the result of a tendency to see him in the light of other uneasy Shakespearean rulers and heroes. Yet, though Henry's difficulty may resemble that of Hamlet or Brutus (or even John), his expression of it is not like theirs, in that it is straightforward and not tortured.[18] But neither is it glib.

Three main problems seem to confront Henry: the rebellion, the separate but related problem of the "crooked byways" by which he came to the throne, and the problem of Hal's apparent prodigality. The last absorbs him more than the others. His most important scene, III.ii, at the center of the play, is the crisis of this problem, to which he here relates the other two.

In this "private conference" with Hal, Henry is as usual direct and forthright. His very way of opening the scene,

> Lords, give us leave; the Prince of Wales and I
> Must have some private conference; but be near at
> hand
> For we shall presently have need of you,
> (ll. 1–3)

twice issuing a command and then giving his reason for it, is a characteristic[19] kind of plain dealing that distinguishes him par-

---

[17]This view of Henry is not entirely orthodox. Some find him guilty of devious circumlocution in the opening scene. My view accords more with that of J. Dover Wilson, who says of Henry's first speech that "The guile that many detect in the speech is not intended. "(*1H4, New Cambridge Shakespeare,* p. 114). The fact that Henry does not soliloquize in *1H4* gives leeway for some range of opinion.

[18]Here again, as with Richard's soliloquylike speech, we touch on the question of the means available to the author. It might be argued that Shakespeare at this stage in his career was simply *unable* to create a tortured expression of difficulty. But even supposing this to be the case, I think this is another case of his making the very limitations of his art functional and significant.

[19]As at, for example, I.iii.14 ff. and V.iv.1.

ticularly from Richard, who was little inclined to justify his commands.

Henry then turns to Hal and comes directly to the point:

> I know not whether God will have it so
> For some displeasing service I have done,
> That in his secret doom out of my blood
> He'll breed revengement and a scourge for me;
> But thou dost in thy passages of life
> Make me believe that thou art only mark'd
> For the hot vengeance and the rod of heaven,
> To punish my mistreadings.
>   (ll. 4–11)

This is his first address to his son, and it is an expression of considerable displeasure. Even so there is a fairness and re-straint in the form of the speech, for Henry's overall speech act here is a request that his hypothesis be disproved by Hal.

Hal does not accede to this request in his reply. Rather he suggests that he has been partly misrepresented "By smiling pickthanks and base newsmongers," though admitting to some fault, for which he asks pardon. But Henry's pardon is not to be had so easily: "*God* pardon thee!" he said, "yet let *me* wonder, Harry, / At thy affections" (italics mine). He states the case against Hal in another way, the obverse of Hal's "rude society":

> thou . . .
> . . . art almost an alien to the hearts
> Of all the court and princes of my blood
>   (ll. 32–35)

a reticent expression of his own disappointed wish for his son's company that is moving and characteristic.

Henry then proceeds to advise and warn Hal, arguing from his own experience:

> Had I so lavish of my presence been,
> So common-hackney'd in the eyes of men,
> So stale and cheap to vulgar company,
> Opinion, that did help me to the crown,
> Had still kept loyal to possession,
> And left me in reputeless banishment,
> A fellow of no mark nor likelihood.
>   (ll. 39–45)

Clearly there are limitations and even error inherent in Henry's giving so much weight to the wooing of "opinion"; but it is also clear that Henry is giving sincere advice, the best he can. And it is impressive for this reticent and "silent king" so to describe and reveal himself. He then describes the "skipping king," Richard, "enfeoffed to popularity." This, too, clearly has limitations, but it is also remarkable because in *R2*, while Richard characterized him repeatedly, he gave nothing approaching such a characterization of the king. He then tells the reason for this long description of Richard: "in that very line, Harry, standest thou."

As the speech concludes, Henry's own immediate and personal feeling, which arose but was restrained at the beginning, comes completely to the surface:

> And in that very line, Harry, standest thou,
> For thou hast lost thy princely privilege
> With vile participation. Not an eye
> But is a-weary of thy common sight,
> Save mine, which hath desir'd to see thee more,
> Which now doth that I would not have it do,
> Make blind itself with foolish tenderness.
> (ll. 85–91)

This moves Hal to do more than ask for pardon. He says

> I shall hereafter, my thrice-gracious lord
> Be more myself.
> (ll. 92–93)

This is a promise or vow, but it is inexplicit and vague, and does not satisfy Henry, who acknowledges it only by pointing out that it is unfulfilled:

> For all the world
> As thou art to this hour was Richard then
> When I from France set foot at Ravenspurgh,
> And even as I was then is Percy now.
> (ll. 93–96)

He goes on to describe Hotspur, his renown and the threat he poses to the throne. "And what say you to this," he asks, but, receiving no reply or expecting none, continues,

> Percy, Northumberland,
> The Archbishop's Grace of York, Douglas, Mortimer,
> Capitulate against us and are up.
>
> (ll. 118–20)

But in a characteristic movement[20] he breaks this off to question the very value of his speaking:

> But wherefore do I tell these news to thee?
> Why, Harry, do I tell thee of my foes,
> Which art my nearest and dearest enemy?
>
> (ll. 121–23)

Finally he ends the speech with a strong rhetorical elaboration of this characterization of Hal as his "dearest enemy."

Now Hal responds with a very particular promise to "redeem all this on Percy's head," making the illocutionary force of this explicit in a ceremonial performative, "This in the name of God I promise here," and in referring to it as "this vow."

Having achieved his end, Henry expresses his satisfaction with characteristic terseness:

> A hundred rebels die in this —
> Thou shalt have charge and sovereign trust herein.
>
> (ll. 160–61)

Blunt enters, and the scene concludes with Henry laying businesslike plans for meeting the rebels.

While one can thus follow Henry's speech action and try to describe its significant features, in this scene and elsewhere the king has comparatively little to say *about* language and speech. Nevertheless, if we observe most of his references to language here — "conference," "tell me," "What say you to this," and "But wherefore do I tell these news to thee" — a fairly definite category seems to emerge. Henry's attention, it seems, is not so much directed to *language* as to *speech*, more particularly to interaction in speech, to "converse." One can describe the scene in general terms as Henry's inducing Hal to converse with him. Earlier with Hotspur, he does just the opposite when he commands him not to speak of Mortimer; but the category of his references to language is the same: there too his mind is on interaction.

---

[20]As at, for example, I.i.27–29, 90.

There is, further, one particular way in which Henry, in this scene and generally, is "silent" about language. He does not make his speech acts explicit, as, say, Hal does with his promise in the same scene. Henry's inexplicitness vis à vis his speech action is in sharp contrast to Richard's characteristic explicitness. In ceremonies speech acts typically are explicit, so that quality of Richard's contributes to the ceremonial quality of his speech; by contrast, Henry's inexplicit speech action seems nonceremonial. But the difference, and its relation to the feature of direction of address, can be given a more precise formulation than seems possible with the rather vague, if accurate, term "ceremonial."

As explained in the Introduction, a given type of speech act such as promising may be performed either inexplicitly (I will do X") or explicitly ("I promise to do X"). Either way, a promise is made for (to, on) the addressee—the "second person." That is, the promise is given to the person(s) (who may be referred to by second-person pronouns, vocatives, etc.) *to whom* the promiser is speaking. And it is given *exclusively* to that person. "You" defines and limits the recipient of the action.

But *the making explicit* of an act may be done for (to, on) hearers *other* than the person addressed (i.e., the "third person"), so that with explicit illocutionary acts (performatives) there can in a sense be two directions of address: the basic act directed toward the second person, and the explicitness toward the third. A pair of examples make clear what I mean by this odd-sounding formulation.

(1) Why, in a marriage ceremony, does the minister say "I hereby pronounce . . ." rather than something like "You are now man and wife"? Either way he would be successfully and nondefectively pronouncing the addressees man and wife. Nor is there any possible ambiguity needing to be cleared up. Is his explicitness, then, merely decorative? Surely the minister is explicit at least partly for the sake of the "dearly beloved . . . gathered . . . together" whom he addressed earlier in the ceremony. As the "you" are being pronounced man and wife, the congregation is being made to witness the act by the explicitness directed to them. In the way the congregation not merely attends but also participates; the ceremony is being performed for them as well as for the bride and groom, since the

state of matrimony initiated by it has a public as well as a private dimension.

Such a rationale is, I think, involved in the typical explicitness of other ceremonies and partly explains the "ceremonial" quality of Richard's characteristically explicit speech action. But it is not only ceremonies that take advantage of the possible dual directedness of performatives. For instance,

(2) In court a defendant being cross-examined exclaims "I deny what you're suggesting! I deny that I was there!" doing explicitly what he could have done inexplicitly ("What you're suggesting isn't true! I wasn't there!"). The basic act of denial is directed at—is done to—the "you," the attorney being addressed. But the explicitness, which might be quite superfluous if only the attorney were involved, is at least partly for the sake of the judge and jury—to emphasize for them the nature of the speech act.

What the two examples have in common, of course, is explicitness for the sake of a third-person witness or audience. Now, while explicitness is not necessarily so directed, it *may* be, whereas the basic illocutionary act is necessarily directed only toward the second-person addressee. [21] Understanding this difference, I think, allows one to get at the significance of the contrast between Richard's explicitness and Henry's inexplicitness.

Richard's speech action, as we have seen, is soliloquylike in its lack of markers for direction of address, so that often he is not talking definitely *to*, not interacting with, anyone. This is to say that the illocutionary acts he performs are typically undirected: there is no "second person" to (for, on) whom the act is done. Many of the kinds of illocutionary acts he performs (defining, stating, etc.) are especially suited to this directionlessness—in

[21]Both Austin and Searle use the fact of the explicit-inexplicit dimension as evidence for further arguments, but neither is much concerned with the *function* of explicitness, though Austin does address the question, as in *How to Do Things with Words*, p. 72, where he explains the development of explicit performatives in these terms: "sophistication and development of social forms and procedures will necessitate clarification" of the nature of the illocutionary act in question. My analysis of explicitness in illocutionary acts grew out of a consideration of Austin's article on "Pretending" (*Philosophical Papers*, pp. 201–19). Since in Chapter 6 I make further use of it, I have presented it at some length here.

contrast to acts such as warning or threatening which are almost inconceivable without a definite direction of address. Yet, typically Richard's undirected action is explicit. And necessarily, in the absence of a second person, this explicitness is of the sort directed toward an audience. To put this peculiar state of affairs another way: Richard's explicit undirected speech is designed to prevent its hearers from acting and to make them serve as witness or audience.

With Henry, these priorities are reversed. The definite direction of address of his speech manifests the directedness of his illocutionary acts performed on, to, for the "you" addressed. Thus his action amounts to *inter*action with other characters, as Richard's did not. Now, while this sort of directed speech action *could* be as explicit as Richard's undirected speech action, Henry's is not. And, in the context of Richard's example, Henry's characteristic inexplicitness is significant. It seems to mark Henry as being little concerned with a third-person audience for his action, little inclined to show his action to such an audience. Thus one can say that his directed inexplicit speech is designed to make its hearers react and interact, and perhaps to prevent them from standing as witness or audience.

This carries the opposition between Henry and Richard to an unearthly neatness, but schematizations may as well be neat, and this one usefully covers more than the sort of linguistic features from which it is abstracted. Henry's advice to Hal that he avoid showing himself to the public, for instance, is a correlate of the inexplicitness of his speech acts; that here he has no soliloquy is a correlate of the directedness of his speech acts; and that his crucial scene is a private conference is a correlate of both.

VII

Richard's perplexity about the absolute nature of language and his would-be divine speech is largely abandoned in *1H4*, and new ways of conceiving of and using language are operative.

There are, to be sure, in the play various echoes of Richard's dilemma; but they are relatively fragmentary and simplistic. For

Hotspur, "honor" so unquestionably names an essence or universal that he can speak of that universal as if it were an object to be plucked from the palefaced moon; he thus displays a simpler, more naive, and extreme realism than Richard ever did. Falstaff, conversely, in saying that "honor" is air, shows a kind of nominalism more simplified and extreme than Richard's.

Hotspur's realism and Falstaff's nominalism are, however, not the most interesting and important points to note about their respective languages. More crucial is that the name, the word "honor," presents no problem to either of them. For Henry's realm is not one in which questions about universals or essences much matter. Language is being used in too many ways, in too many struggles, for a notion like "name" to be dwelt on or brooded over.

It is being used not, as with Richard, as a material for the construction of verbal objects, but as a medium for action and interaction. Henry's "silence," his reticence and lack of explicitness, reflect a direction of attention almost exclusively toward speech rather than language. And the same direction of attention appears in his allowing of forcible engagement in verbal interaction (as he does with Hal) or his refusal to allow it (as with Hotspur).

Henry's conception of language extends beyond the court to the entire realm. Whether aggressive or playful, the speech in *1H4* is always lively and active. It is more obviously so outside the court—in the rebel camp or at the tavern—because there we have a continually shifting "control" of interchange, whereas Henry assumes almost complete control of his interchanges. It is, in any case, the activeness of the speech that makes "control" important throughout the play (as it was not in *R2*).

Henry's language, then, and not Richard's, is the proper context in which to examine Hotspur's and Falstaff's language, and Hal's. Hotspur's speech is lively as can be; but it tends toward mere activity as he overrides real or imaginary interlocutors as if ignoring or trying to ignore what distinguishes verbal action from such nonverbal actions as killing six or seven dozen Scots at a breakfast. His impatience with other speakers and with other manners of speech seems, finally, to reflect a dislike of communication.

The case is different with Falstaff. In *2H4* deafness will become his *modus operandi,* and even here he does say that "an old lord . . . rated me . . . but I marked him not, and yet he talked very wisely" (I.ii.81–84). But in *1H4* Falstaff's speech constitutes more genuinely communicative interaction than Hotspur's. The peculiar flaw in Falstaff here is not so much a refusal to engage his interlocutors as a refusal to take this engagement seriously—a refusal to converse responsibly.

Hal shows neither Hotspur's nor Falstaff's limitation. In his characteristic promising, for instance, and especially in the "solemn vow" he makes to Henry, his speech action is directed, communicative, responsible, and consequential. Furthermore, Hal, in his learning of tongues and in the widely varying manners in which he speaks, shows himself coming to grips with the variety of languages, with a fact that is to assume increasingly greater importance as the tetralogy continues.

CHAPTER THREE

❈ 2 *Henry IV*

The "justling time" of *1H4*, justling with rebellion and the struggle for control, with comedy and heroic action, all manifesting the vigor and release attendant on Richard's deposition, is followed by "th'unquiet time" (*2H4*, I.ii.149), "the scambling and unquiet time" (*H5*, I.i.4) of *2H4*, in which the graver effects of the deposition are felt throughout the realm. The rebels here, much less eager to justle than was Hotspur, find themselves

> enforc'd from our most quiet . . .
> By the rough torrent of occasion.
>
> (IV.i.71–72)

Mrs. Quickly's "be quiet, 'tis very late i' faith" (II.iv.158–59) voices a general wish, the same that underlies Henry's prediction that the crown "shall descend with better quiet" (IV.v.187) to Hal. The presenter of the unquiet time is Rumour, whose "office is / To noise abroad" (Ind.28–29). His opening lines,

> Open your ears; for which of you will stop
> The vent of hearing when loud Rumour speaks?
> I, from the Orient to the drooping West,
> Making the wind my post-horse, still unfold
> The acts commenced on this ball of earth.
> Upon my tongues continual slanders ride,
> The which in every language I pronounce,
> Stuffing the ears of men with false reports,
>
> (Ind.1–8)

are a fitting point of departure for discussion of the topic of language in the play.

As will be seen throughout the following, my understanding of the play, especially of the mood and tone and of the importance of the theme of time, has been aided and influenced most by L. C. Knights's essay "Time's Subjects: the Sonnets and *2 Henry IV*,"[1] which is, as A. R. Humphreys states, "one of the few first-rate discussions of the play."[2]

1. *"The which in every language I pronounce, . . ."*

In these words of "Rumour *painted full of tongues*" the Babel theme of the proliferation of tongues enters vigorously and more explicitly than before in the tetralogy. And since it is enunciated by a presenter rather than a character in the main drama, it carries special authority: in the world of this play the fall of the tower, the variety of languages, is an accomplished fact, a necessity. And the characters accept it and meet it as a necessity more than they did in *1H4*.

The most obvious way to meet the necessity is to become polyglot and to translate. This is attempted in various ways and degrees, and in fact it becomes a metaphor for action in general:

> Wherefore do you ill translate yourself
> Out of the speech of peace that bears such grace
> Into the harsh and boist'rous tongue of war. . . ?
> (IV.i.47–49)

This is Westmoreland accusing the archbishop of taking improper advantage of the possibility of translating between tongues. Hal, on the other hand, (according to Warwick)

> but studies his companions
> Like a strange tongue, wherein, to gain the language,
> 'Tis needful that the most immodest word
> Be look'd upon and learnt; which once attain'd,

---

[1] In *Some Shakespearean Themes*.

[2] New Arden *2H4*, p.liii, n. 2. Humphreys's own introductory commentary has been helpful to me. I would also mention here two of the works cited in the bibliography below to which this chapter is especially indebted: Richard Knowles's "Unquiet and the Double Plot of *2H4*" and Arthur Sewell's splendid *Character and Society in Shakespeare*.

Your Highness knows, comes to no further use
But to be known and hated.
(IV.iv.68–73)

Here in Hal's polyglotism, which might have seemed merely
playful in *1H4*, we find the conscientious sense of responsibility
that before showed up mainly in his promising. A knowledge of
tongues begins to appear essential in the new ideal he represents. And in Warwick's praise there is the hope that Hal will be
able to redeem the proliferated tongues that resulted from
Richard's heavenscaling.

What is true of most of Shakespeare's briefer metaphors
seems true of these extended and deliberate ones: they can bear
considerable pressure of interpretation. We can, for instance,
reverse them. If characteristic behavior and action is a kind of
language, so language is a kind of characteristic behavior and
action. And we may press even further and find in these
metaphors the suggestion that to speak is to speak not simply
English, not simply, say, a 1590s London dialect, but an idiolect:
one's own unique characteristic language. So that to speak at all
is to manifest what differentiates one from all others, to give
oneself away. Yet, on the other hand, these metaphors also
suggest the likelihood of one's self-expression being misun-
derstood, the difficulty of communication, of crossing the barriers of idiolect. A good deal of the action of the play consists of
the various characters' ways of dealing with this state of affairs.

At Gaultree, for instance, in the interchange of performatives

Archbishop. I take your princely word for these
. redresses.
Lancaster. I give it you, and will maintain my word
(IV.ii.66–67)

the matter comes to a head. For John's success depends on the
rebels' mistaking him by mis-taking his word. His word is good:
he will fulfill his promise, but the rebels err in interpreting that
promise freely, charitably, and to their advantage.

The case is similar with Hal and his Boar's Head companions
insofar as they, especially Falstaff, misinterpret him. However
their misinterpretation seems less defensible than the rebels',

and Hal seems less culpable than John. This is because the rebels have misread John's *silence,* while Falstaff and Poins have misread Hal's *speech.* That is, John tells the best that he will do but is silent about the worst, whereas Hal clearly tells or implies the worst: "I do, I will,"[3] and "What a disgrace it is to me to remember thy name! or to know thy face tomorrow!" Of course with his father, and with the nation in general, Hal is silent through much of the *H4* plays about the best that he will do; his promise of a reformation that will "show more goodly" is made in soliloquy.

Yet even after a comparison with those who do not keep promises (most of the rebels) and with John who keeps promises with unchivalrous literalness, there is a residue of unpleasantness about Hal's procedure. He seems wilfully to allow Falstaff and Poins to misinterpret him; he knows them all, and presumably knows that they misread his open and direct disclaimers, and presumably he could make them see, if he would. One might argue that in a world of tongues there must necessarily be some misinterpretation, and that it is the unpleasantness of this fact that we feel in Hal's scenes with Poins and Falstaff. It could be argued that Hal would be less admirable if he had not been presented with the problem, if Shakespeare had either made him unconscious of it or surrounded him with perfect interpreters and so placed him in a kind of unfallen world.

The issues I have just been discussing are a part of the Babel theme, but they hang together sufficiently to deserve a topic heading of their own, "the idea of idiolect," the idea of speech as necessarily occurring in a unique and, for Shakespeare, meaningfully characteristic language. Under the rubric of "style" the idea has been of great importance in literature and literary criticism; indeed its ramifications are vast. I shall later (in chapters 5 and 6) return to the matter, considering it in relation to the idea of drama. Here I would only suggest that, coming to the fore as it does in *2H4,* the idea of idiolect carries to an extreme in the tetralogy the problem of the proliferation of tongues. Even Lady Mortimer's Welsh implied a community, but in *2H4* there is no mention of such shared, named tongues.

---

[3]While it is possible that Falstaff does not hear this, the point is that Hal says it.

Every man speaks his own. We have reached the opposite extreme from the sort of undivided universal language Richard seemed to envision.

This state of affairs is manifested even in the Induction; indeed it explains what on the surface might seem an odd inconsistency. That Rumour pronounces his slanders "in every language" might seem irrelevant since there is no French or Welsh or Latin or even Irish or Scottish dialect in the play.[4] The explanation, I would hold, is that Rumour's "languages" are idiolects; that his tongues signify at once the multitude of individual speakers *and* their individual ways of speaking. The normal ambiguity in "tongue," between (1) the organ and faculty of speech and (2) a language distinct from others, collapses, or threatens to collapse.

The same collapsing ambiguity appears in Falstaff's elaborate figure, "I have a whole school of tongues in this belly of mine . . ." (IV.iii.18), which allies him with Rumour as a representative of the world of proliferated tongues. He continues, "and not a tongue of them all speaks any other word but my name" (ll. 19–20), so presenting another version of the vitiation involved. (Here again—as with the speech on honor in *1H4*—Falstaff comes across as an uncanny vestige of Richard, in this case a Richard who, though finally recognizing the fact of the variety of tongues, is unable to use language for anything at all other than pronouncing his own name.)

The play calls up varying images or assessments of the world of tongues tending toward idiolect. It is a confusion, a chaos like that summoned in Northumberland's

> Let heaven kiss earth! Now let not Nature's hand
> Keep the wild flood confin'd! Let order die!
> (I.i.153–54)

It is "a tempest of commotion" (II.iv.360), a "still-discordant wav'ring multitude" (Ind.19) for Rumour to noise abroad in. It is ruled by chance, accident, and fortune,[5] a Babel of accusations

---

[4]There are three moments of muddled foreign language—Latin (V.v.28) and Romance (II.iv.177 and V.v.96)—all provided by Pistol.

[5]Chance has almost literally replaced the God of *R2* who, it was supposed, would determine the victory in the tournament between Bolingbroke and Mow-

like "You speak, Lord Mowbray, now you know not what" (IV.i.130) in which words are turned to swords (IV.ii.10). It is a world in which Pistol, with his near meaningless rant and exclamations like "let the welkin roar" (II.iv.165), is perhaps the typical speaker.

On the other hand, however, we have a state of affairs in which each man can have his own private version of Richard's Edenic linguistic absolutism. This view of the situation seems implicit in the rich pastoralism of the play, in the Boar's Head where Mrs. Quickly, believing herself "in good name and fame with the very best" (II.iv.73–74), blithely speaks her idiosyncratic language, and especially in the Gloucestershire scenes, where Silence can sing and be merry.[6]

2. *"Upon my tongues continual slanders ride*
. . . .
Stuffing the ears of men with false reports."

Reporting—communication of facts—is one of the most frequently mentioned and frequently occurring speech acts in the play. Contrasting with the prophecy and magical ceremonial performatives of *R2*, its prevalence marks a general secularization, rationalization, and simplification of the operative conceptions of language.

It was of course conflicting reports, in the form of accusations about the death of Woodstock, that set the tetralogy in motion. Richard's initial refusal to allow any sort of verification in his court created an atmosphere favorable to the spread of rumors, the effects of which Richard suffered in the catastrophic dispersal of his forces resulting from the rumor of his death. In *1H4* false reports are promulgated by the "father of lies," Sir John Falstaff. Now, in *2H4*, Rumour rules down to "the blunt monster with uncounted heads, / The still-discordant wav'ring multitude" (Ind.18–19); and among the higher-ranking society the

---

bray. Now, in *2H4*, Westmoreland says of that contest, "Who knows on whom Forture would then have smil'd?"

[6] Could the Edenic quality of the Boar's Head and Gloucestershire scenes have to do with the odd discussions of apples in both places (II.iv.1–10 and V.iii.1–3)?

effects of rumor are suffered most by those now taking Richard's part, the rebels in the opening scenes of the play.[7]

In this kingdom with an ailing king and a weary prince the search for truth is nothing like as ambitious as Richard's struggle to say who and what he is. Here, discovering the truth about brute events seems all that can be hoped for, and even this truth is not sought very energetically. Two versions of Hotspur's death[8] are current which never come into conflict. In passages like the interchange

> *Morton.* I hear for certain, and dare speak the truth,
>   The gentle Archbishop of York is up . . .
>   . . . .
>
> *Northumberland.* I knew of this before, but, to speak the
>   truth,
>   This present grief had wip'd it from my mind
>   (I.i.188–211)

we find the word "truth" itself subject to peculiarly lame and vacuous uses, which mark a "heavy descension" (II.ii.166) to a world in which "Pistol speaks naught but truth" (V.v.38).

In such a climate the pervasive sense of retrospect is especially poignant. With news so illusory and disheartening, the characters seem to take refuge in reporting what is already known about the past. This play, probably more than any other of Shakespeare's, is full of quiet descriptions of events that happened long before the action begins. It goes on at every level of society—Henry and Warwick talk about occurrences during Richard's reign, Falstaff turns out to have been in his youth "page to Thomas Mowbray, Duke of Norfolk," Silence remembers that Shallow was called "lusty Shallow" at Clement's Inn. The mood ranges from the relatively sweet Gloucestershire retrospect, through Henry's troubled wondering at "the revolution of the times" (III.i.46), to Northumberland's

---

[7]At one point, what may be an indirect allusion to the Tower of Babel is associated with the rebels. In I.iii Lord Bardolph, discussing their enterprise, makes a fairly extensive allusion to the Parable of the Builder (*Luke* 14:28–30), which begins, "For which of you minding *to buylde a towre*, sitteth not down before, and counteth the cost, whether he haue sufficient to performe it" (Genevan, italics mine).

[8]The truth, and the version that credits Falstaff and therefore leads Colevile to surrender (IV.iii).

> Fair daughter, you do draw my spirits from me
> With new lamenting ancient oversights
>   (II.iii.46–47)

with its bitter hopelessness.

Such reporting of events that comprise "history," from the relatively distant past, intermingles with the also frequent reporting of more recent or contemporary events, that is, "news" or "tidings." Together they give special prominence to the occasional references to prophecy, the "reporting" of future events. These references to prophecy are mostly associated with Henry, as though now, with the justling that followed his ascension to the throne having passed, something of the magical and ominous linguistic atmosphere of Richard's realm has returned to haunt him. He quotes at length from Richard's "words, now prov'd a prophecy" (III.i.69–77). And he dies vacuously fulfilling a prophecy, through an accident of naming, in "Jerusalem." Afterwards, Hal's

> I survive . . .
> · · · · · · · ·
> To frustrate prophecies
>   (V.ii.125–27)

is a sharp and clear announcement of a reigning conception of language free from the old difficulties of the preceding reigns. Immersed in the destructive element—learning "gross terms" and being traduced by rumor—Hal has nevertheless frustrated prophecy in keeping his private promise to falsify men's hopes.

One type of reporting the past deserves special attention. This is the quotation of what someone has said, usually before the play's opening, which also seems to occur more frequently here than elsewhere in Shakespeare. Direct quotation is a very peculiar kind of report, that of a speech act that reenacts the "locutionary act" reported; it would thus seem to be the most precise, accurate, and complete kind of report possible. (The same holds true to a lesser extent for indirect quotation, depending on how indirect it is.) To report or describe any other sort of action is almost certainly to interpret, to be imprecise and incomplete. But reports of the form "'X' said 'Y'" are complete as far as they go: there is nothing more we can ask about the act since it has been exactly reperformed by the reporter. The questions we may yet have are, to use Austinian terms, about higher-level acts performed at the same time: what was the speaker doing in saying "Y," what was the illocutionary and perlocutionary act and, more generally, what was the speech-situation. These levels of reportage involve interpretation, of course, and if this is a drawback it is one that society must put up with. But in *2H4* the mood of disillusionment is such that the characters seem inclined to retrench, to give up the attempt to deal with the higher levels of speech action and to take comfort in reporting mere words.

This reduction is perhaps most apparent in Mrs. Quickly's comically and rather pathetically careful quotation

> I was before Master Tisick the debuty t'other day, and,
> as he said to me—'twas no longer ago than
> Wednesday last, i' good faith—'Neighbour Quickly,'
> says he—Master Dumb our minister was by
> then—'Neighbour Quickly,' says he, 'receive those that
> are civil, for,' said he, 'you are in an ill name'—now a
> said so, I can tell whereupon. 'For,' says he, 'you are
> an honest woman, and well thought on, therefore take
> heed what guests you receive; receive,' says he, 'no
> swaggering companions.'
>   (II.iv.82–92)

The insistent accuracy of this word-for-word reportage is clearly fatuous, and made more so by the reporter's frequent ignorance of the very meaning of words.

The sense of retrenchment and reduction, comic in Quickly's quotation, is poignant when we find it in the king himself. With an unlikely echo of Quickly's noting particulars of the occasion and repeating "he said . . . says he," Henry quotes Richard:

> But which of you was by—
> [To Warwick] You, cousin Nevil, as I may remember—
> When Richard, with his eye brimful of tears,
> ·
> Did speak these words, now prov'd a prophecy?
> 'Northumberland, thou ladder by the which

> My cousin Bolingbroke ascends my throne'
> (Though then, God knows, I had no such intent
> But that necessity so bow'd the state
> That I and greatness were compell'd to kiss)
> 'The time shall come'—thus did he follow it—
> 'The time will come, that foul sin, gathering head
> Shall break into corruption'—so went on. . . .
>
> (III.i.65–77)

The remarkable similarity of procedure in Henry's and Quickly's quotation marks the pervasiveness—from the top to the bottom of the society—of a helpless reduction to the mere careful repetition of words.

The most frequent use of quotation is for the transmission of rumor and news, in which case we have reports of reports (perhaps even of reports, etc.).

> The posts come tiring on,
> And not a man of them brings other news
> Than they have learnt of me
>
> (Ind.37–39)

announces Rumour, and the play opens with conflicting reports, in the form of indirect quotations, of the battle of Shrewsbury. Morton, an eyewitness, arrives, but before he can report, Northumberland quotes him in advance:

> This thou wouldst say, 'Your son did thus and thus;
> Your brother thus; so fought the noble Douglas'—
>
> (I.i.76–77)

Morton in turn admonishes Northumberland by quoting his own pre-Shrewsbury words to him (ll. 167–68, 175), and then encourages him with a quotation of better news (ll. 188–90). So throughout the play quotation is a vehicle for news and, even more, for reactions to news.

With regard to quotation, as to prophecy, Hal sets himself apart from most of the other characters. In IV.v, he surprisingly and interestingly misquotes something he has said a few lines earlier. Indeed "misquote" with its suggestion of an attempt to quote accurately, is hardly the word, for the words Hal ascribes to himself,

> I spake unto this crown as having sense,
> And thus upbraided it: 'The care on thee depending
> Hath fed upon the body of my father;
> Therefore thou best of gold art worst of gold . . . ,'
>   (IV.v.157–60)

are quite different from those we have just heard him utter. Sigurd Burckhardt is, I think, right in his belief that "this is one of the many instances where Shakespeare does something odd because he wants to startle us into paying close attention."[9] Burckhardt finds that the difference in the content of Hal's two speeches elucidates Shakespeare's conception of kingship. But what I find interesting is that the mere fact of the discrepancy shows Hal radically high-handed where others are most timid—in his attitude toward the word. I say "high-handed" rather than "double-dealing" because I agree with Burckhardt that we cannot take Hal for a hypocrite and liar. Considering his other behavior in the tetralogy, I think we must assume that what he says to his father is true. That is, we must assume that for him the original utterance and the quoted one are in some sense the same. And this is to say that Hal looks very deeply beneath the surface of speech action.[10]

It is also to distinguish him from the play's other notably inaccurate reporter of speech acts. Falstaff lies in *1H4*, but in *2H4* there seems to be a certain specificity in his lying. His false reports here tend to be about other people's speech acts, to their discredit. Inasmuch as he is especially concerned with what people say, he manifests the play's general tendency to retreat from general problems of speech action—not to mention general problems of action or of language—and to focus on the mere locutionary act, the act of saying such-and-such a thing. And inasmuch as his reports are of the acts of others, to their discredit and false, he is the play's most prominent practitioner of the act named by Rumour, slander. It is slander now, instead of cowardice, that he must contrive to defend: he had dispraised Hal before the wicked

[9]*Shakespearean Meanings*, p. 163.
[10]At V.ii.107ff., Hal has another interesting quotation, of his father's assessment of the Lord Chief Justice.

> that the wicked might not fall in love with thee: in
> which doing, I have done the part of a careful friend
> and a true subject
>
> (II.iv.317–19)

which defense involves further dispraise ("the wicked"), of
Quickly, Tearsheet, Bardolph, and the page Hal has given him.
He also slanders Poins and Quickly on other occasions.[11] Indeed
enough slander rides on Falstaff's tongue, or his "whole school
of tongues," to raise the possibility that he is the main action's
embodiment of the presenter, Rumour.[12]

3. *"Open your ears; for which of you will stop*
The vent of hearing when loud Rumour speaks?"

These opening words of Rumour's announce what is to be a
major issue in Shakespeare's handling of speech action in *2H4*,
the subject of deafness. A concentration on the inability and,
more, the refusal to hear or listen is another manifestation of the
play's general retreat to a concern with the most elementary
features of speech action. For if speech is not heard it is rendered
ineffectual; its basic purpose is removed and communication is
impossible. In Austin's terms, a locutionary act (e.g., the act of
uttering the sentence "I urge you to X") can still be performed if
the speech is not heard, but there is no possibility of performing the corresponding illocution (e.g., the act of urging) and
perlocution (e.g., the act of persuading). Thus deafness is a
peculiarly vicious attack on the institution of language, for it, so
to speak, kills the soul of language without harming its body.
Furthermore, by eliminating communication, deafness, like the
extreme sense of idiolect, eliminates community.

Deafness is thematically important in the previous plays of
the tetralogy, indeed as early as the opening scene in which
Richard agrees to listen to "the boist'rous late appeal, / Which
then our leisure would not let us hear." A consequence of
Richard's special linguistic *Weltanschauung* is a general deafness
to the speakers around him. Henry IV turns a deaf ear to

---

[11]Quickly at II.i.102–3, Poins at II.ii.12–122, and also various and sundry
others such as Master Dommelton the tailor (I.ii.45–48).

[12]I have searched, unsuccessfully, for evidence of the two roles being played
by the same actor.

Hotspur's complaints and demands, and then Hotspur is accused of "tying thine ear to no tongue but thine own." But in *2H4* deafness is dealt with more extensively, and there is also a qualitative change in the presentation of the problem. With Richard and with Hotspur the deafness seems involuntary; but that discussed in *2H4* is wilful and deliberate:

> *Chief Justice.* I think you are fallen into the disease, for
>   you hear not what I say to you.
> *Falstaff.* Very well, my lord, very well. Rather, and't
>   please you, it is the disease of not listening, the
>   malady of not marking, that I am troubled withal.
>   (I.ii.117–21)

Of course in this scene Falstaff does listen, as well as hear, very well. His deafness amounts to an "ignoring," a refusal to acknowledge that communication has taken place.[13]

And this refusal of Falstaff's, this "deafness," is manifested in his own speech:

> *Ch. Just.* Sir John, I sent for you before your expedition
>   to Shrewsbury.
> *Fal.* And't please your lordship, I hear his Majesty is
>   returned with some discomfort from Wales.
> *Ch. Just.* I talk not of his Majesty. You would not come
>   when I sent for you.
> *Fal.* And I hear, moreover, his Highness is fallen into
>   this same whoreson apoplexy.
>   (I.ii.100–107)

He does not reply to the Lord Chief Justice's speeches, but continues as if the LCJ had not spoken.

These interchanges occur in Falstaff's and the LCJ's first scene. "Deafness" is not subsequently discussed so explicitly, but as a feature of the speech action it continues to be important, especially in the relations between these two characters, which constitute the play's most extensively dramatized and complete agon. To trace this feature in their interactions is to see in detail

---

[13]Falstaff has been troubled with "the malady of not marking" at least once in *1H4*, at II.iv.11off., where he does not hear Hal. Also in that play he mentions that "an old lord . . . rated me . . . but I marked him not, and yet he talked very wisely" (*1H4*, I.ii.81–84), as noted above (Chapter 2, p. 88).

how Shakespeare characterizes by speech action; and it is also to
see again what I hope to have demonstrated with the earlier
plays: that there is in the tetralogy a close relation between (1)
what is said *about* language and (2) the speech action itself. The
agon between Falstaff and the LCJ comprises a remarkably clear,
extensive, and consistent example of the dramaturgical embodiment of an important language theme.

As A. R. Humphreys notes about the two characters' first
encounter, "This confrontation, and the fact that the Lord Chief
Justice is not worsted, are pointers to the play's course."[14] Indeed the procedure in this scene by which Falstaff and the LCJ
engage in conversation ironically mirrors a similar procedure in
the scene of Falstaff's judgment. There the sequence is (1)
Falstaff tries to engage Hal, (2) Hal declines and instructs the
LCJ to reply, (3) Falstaff persists, refusing to deal with the LCJ,
(4) Hal at last speaks to Falstaff. Here the situation is complicated by the LCJ's servant, but the sequence is basically the
same: (1) the LCJ tries to engage Falstaff, (2) Falstaff declines and
instructs his page to reply, (3) the LCJ persists, refusing to deal
with the page, (4) Falstaff at last speaks to the LCJ.

The complication of the LCJ's servant in this first scene is,
however, worth noting. It means that each antagonist has his
announcer or second by means of whom he first deals with the
other. Thus the beginning of their interaction has a slightly formal and ceremonial quality, perhaps reminiscent of the opening
of the lists in *R2*. It allows the two men to square off.

But from the beginning Falstaff is on the defensive, and his
defense is deafness. At first he will not even hear the LCJ's
servant, and will only deal with him through his page:

> *Servant.* Sir John Falstaff!
> *Falstaff.* Boy, tell him I am deaf.
> *Page.* You must speak louder, my master is deaf.
> (I.ii.65–67)

The page is addressing the LCJ's servant, but the LCJ acknowledges that he has heard,

> *Ch. Just.* I am sure he is, to the hearing of anything
> good

[14]In his note on I.ii.54.S.D.

thus shortening the line of communication by one step and coming closer to Falstaff.

Falstaff then shortens the line by two steps at once, acknowledging that he has heard the servant and addressing him:

> *Servant.* Sir John!
> *Fal.* What! A young knave, and begging!

But this capitulation is itself a defense. Falstaff will speak to the servant but scarcely with him. He postpones dealing with the LCJ by wilfully misunderstanding the servant:

> *Fal.* . . . A young knave, and begging! Is there not
> wars? Is there not employment? Doth the King lack
> subjects? Do not the rebels need soldiers? Though it
> be a shame to be on any side but one, it is worse
> shame to beg than to be on the worst side, were it
> worse than the name of rebellion can tell how to
> make it.
> *Servant.* You mistake me, sir.

Falstaff continues to mistake him until the LCJ moves again to close the gap completely from his side by addressing Falstaff:

> *Ch. Just.* Sir John Falstaff, a word with you.

Falstaff seems to capitulate again. His reply is aggressively impertinent, even perhaps slightly threatening—

> *Fal.* My good lord! God give your worship good time of
> day. I am glad to see your lordship abroad, I heard
> say your lordship was sick. I hope your lordship
> goes abroad by advice; your lordship, though not
> clean past your youth, have yet some smack of age
> in you, some relish of the saltness of time; and I
> most humbly beseech your lordship to have a
> reverend care of your health.

—yet he seems at this juncture to have given up deafness, and so given himself up to communication.

The LCJ ignores Falstaff's impertinence and comes brusquely to the point:

> *Ch. Just.* Sir John, I sent for you before your expedition
> to Shrewsbury.

But in the next interchange it becomes clear that Falstaff's last capitulation was by no means so complete as it seemed, for though he will address the LCJ he will not hear him:

> *Fal.* And't please your lordship, I hear his Majesty is returned with some discomfort from Wales.
> *Ch. Just.* I talk not of his Majesty. You would not come when I sent for you.
> *Fal.* And I hear, moreover, his Highness is fallen into this same whoreson apoplexy.
> *Ch. Just.* Well, God mend him! I pray you let me speak with you.
> *Fal.* This apoplexy, as I take it, is a kind of lethargy, and't please your lordship, a kind of sleeping in the blood, a whoreson tingling.
> *Ch. Just.* What tell you me of it? Be it as it is.
> *Fal.* It hath its original from much grief, from study, and perturbation of the brain; I have read the cause of his effects in Galen, it is a kind of deafness.
> *Ch. Just.* I think you are fallen into the disease, for you hear not what I say to you.

In this situation Falstaff's repeated "I hear" in his first two speeches above is a taunting audacity. His next move is even bolder. He admits in a stroke that his deafness has been wilful, both explicitly, by what he says about himself, and implicitly, by replying directly to the LCJ for the first time:

> *Fal.* Very well, my lord, very well. Rather, and't please you, it is the disease of not listening, the malady of not marking, that I am troubled withal.

The resonant ironies here are very large—Falstaff's description of himself is, for instance, a commentary on the whole course of his relations with Hal.[15] And this audacity, like most of Falstaff's, involves some capitulation. Here he has at last given in to acknowledged communication.

Thereafter in this confrontation Falstaff communicates, but

---

[15]Hal, for his part, has shown himself free of the malady of not marking:

> *Fal.* Dost thou hear me, Hal?
> *Prince.* Ay; and mark thee too, Jack.

(1H4, II.iv.204–5)

his strategy still involves something like deafness in his refusal to heed and admit. Almost the entire remainder of the action repeats the pattern of the next interchange:

> *Ch. Just.* To punish you by the heels would amend the attention of your ears, and I care not if I do become your physician.
>
> *Fal.* I am as poor as Job, my lord, but not so patient. Your lordship may minister the portion of imprisonment to me in respect of poverty; but how I should be so patient to follow your prescriptions, the wise may make some drain of a scruple, or indeed a scruple itself.

That is, the LCJ thrusts with accusation or admonition, and Falstaff parries by dismissing, denying, or wittily playing on the justice's words. Only at the end does Falstaff take the conversational initiative, and then he himself is dismissed:

> *Fal.* Will your lordship lend me a thousand pound to furnish me forth?
>
> *Ch. Just.* Not a penny, not a penny; you are too impatient to bear crosses. Fare you well: commend me to my cousin Westmoreland.
>
> *Exeunt Lord Chief Justice and Servant*

The next encounter occurs when the LCJ comes upon the scene of Mrs. Quickly's attempt to arrest Falstaff (II.i). The LCJ admonishes Falstaff for "brawling" when he should be on his way to York, and he hears Mrs. Quickly's complaint. Then he addresses Falstaff:

> *Ch. Just.* How comes this, Sir John? Fie! what man of good temper would endure this tempest of exclamation? Are you not ashamed to enforce a poor widow to so rough a course to come by her own?
>
> (II.i.78–81)

But Falstaff does not choose to answer the question or even to address the LCJ yet. Instead he speaks to the hostess:

> *Fal.* What is the gross sum that I owe thee?

She replies with a voluminous catalogue of his offenses, ending,

"I put thee now to thy book oath, deny it if thou canst." Moments before it was convenient to be deaf to her; and Falstaff avoids acknowledging her challenge by addressing the LCJ for the first time in this scene, with a slander on the hostess:

> *Fal.* My lord this is a poor mad soul, and she says up
> and down the town that her eldest son is like you.

The kind of deafness evinced here differs from that of the earlier scene, where, with only one interlocutor, Falstaff showed his deafness by exhibiting in his speech a leisurely expository sequence undisturbed by the LCJ's interruptions. Here, with two interlocutors, Falstaff's deafness is less blatant because it is manifested in his addressing either of them when he chooses not to hear the other.

Falstaff takes Mrs. Quickly aside, talks her into withdrawing the action of arrest, and she exits.[16] Meanwhile Gower has arrived with a letter for the LCJ who, after reading it, says, "I have heard better news." He is talking to Gower, or even to himself, but Falstaff hears and asks, "What's the news, my lord?" Now it is Falstaff's turn to speak to deaf ears: not deigning to reply, the LCJ addresses Gower:

> *Ch. Just.* Where lay the King tonight?
> *Gower.* At Basingstoke, my lord.

With a more respectful and propitiatory preface Falstaff tries again:

> *Fal.* I hope, my lord, all's well. What is the news, my
> lord?

only to be met with the same deafness in the LCJ, who continues to address Gower:

> *Ch. Just.* Come all his forces back?
> *Gower.* No, fifteen hundred foot, five hundred horse
> Are march'd up to my Lord of Lancaster,
> Against Northumberland and the Archbishop.

Falstaff tries a more specific question and an expanded honorific:

---

[16]Pliable as she is here, Falstaff later (II.iv.77,80) finds her growing deaf to him (and for her deafness, v. below, p. 109).

> *Fal.* Comes the King back from Wales, my noble lord?

For the third time the LCJ is deaf to Falstaff and continues to address Gower:

> *Ch. Just.* You shall have letters of me presently.
> Come, go along with me, good Master Gower.

Falstaff is reduced to an exclaimed vocative, "My lord!" and at last the LCJ acknowledges him by addressing him: "What's the matter?"

Perhaps galled by so large a dose of his own medicine, Falstaff seizes the opportunity to be deaf again, to ignore the address he has been assiduously seeking, by addressing Gower:

> *Fal.* Master Gower, shall I entreat you with me to
> dinner?

Gower refuses politely, and the LCJ addresses Falstaff again:

> *Ch. Just.* Sir John, you loiter here too long, being you
> are to take soldiers up in the counties as you go.

and again Falstaff shows deafness by addressing Gower:

> *Fal.* Will you sup with me, Master Gower?

But this is rather pitifully fatuous. Gower has already answered this question, and by asking it again thus, Falstaff involuntarily implies that he has not marked the words of the very man he is trying to win away from the justice. The LCJ then addresses Falstaff a third time,

> *Ch. Just.* What foolish master taught you these
> manners, Sir John?

and Falstaff reaches a new level of wilful deformation of the speech-situation when he replies to the LCJ's words but addresses the reply to Gower:

> *Fal.* Master Gower, if they become me not, he was a
> fool that taught them me.[17]

And then, as if satisfied at having contrived to turn a deaf ear as

---

[17]Falstaff here seems to be implying that the LJC taught *him* the manner of not attending!

many times as one was turned to him, he at last addresses the Justice:

> *Fal.* This is the right fencing grace, my lord; tap for tap, and so part fair.

But "tap for tap" as a description of anything more than the simplest mechanics of the interchange is wishful thinking. The LCJ's initial refusal to attend has driven Falstaff to a deafness more fatuous and more hopeless than that of the earlier scene. And he has the last word:

> *Ch. Just.* Now the Lord lighten thee, thou art a great fool.
>
> > > *Exeunt.*

The last two encounters of these antagonists are very brief, but they echo with what has gone before. I have already mentioned the similarities between the scene of Falstaff's first encounter with the LCJ and that of his rejection by Hal. In the latter, Falstaff addresses Hal, who at first refuses to reply, instructing the LCJ to deal with Falstaff:

> *Fal.* God save thee, my sweet boy!
> *King.* My lord Chief Justice, speak to that vain man.
> *Ch. Just.* Have you your wits? Know you what 'tis you speak?
>
> > > (V.v.43–45)

Falstaff however refuses to hear the justice, and addresses Hal again:

> *Fal.* My king! My Jove! I speak to thee, my heart!

whereupon Hal at last replies directly:

> *King.* I know thee not, old man. Fall to thy prayers.

All the vocatives in the agon I have been describing have been polite and formal; at his most exasperated the LCJ has addressed Falstaff as "Sir John." The personal pronouns have also been formal and polite, until the last speech of the earlier scene when the LCJ used the familiar form in "Now the Lord lighten thee, thou art a great fool." It is this pronoun "thee" by which Hal's address to Falstaff here is first manifested, though Falstaff might for a moment suppose the form to be friendly, as before in Hal's address to him, rather than contemptuous. But the magnitude of the king's displeasure stands fully revealed in his shocking, insulting vocative, "old man."

Hal confronts Falstaff here with a deafness more aggressive and absolute than any that the other has had the power to display—he will not permit him even to speak:

> Reply not to me with a fool-born jest.
>
> (V.v.55)

When he has finished speaking to Falstaff he turns directly to the LCJ:

> Be it your charge, my lord,
> To see performed the tenor of my word.
> Set on.
>
> *Exit King with his train.*

The last encounter of Falstaff and the LCJ comes a few lines later:

> *Ch. Just.* Go carry Sir John Falstaff to the Fleet; Take all
>   his company along with him.
> *Fal.* My lord, my lord,—
> *Ch. Just.* I cannot now speak: I will hear you soon. Take
>   them away.
>
> (V.v.91–95)

The justice's victory is complete: with Falstaff he will hear, speak, and be heard at his convenience and choice. But he does not exult. He ameliorates Falstaff's defeat when, in referring to what I have tried to show to be one of the essential terms of their agon, he promises to hear.

While it is in the Falstaff-LCJ agon that deafness is most notably mentioned and most extensively and systematically dramatized, this topic is important elsewhere, too. The archbishop complains that his party "might by no suit gain our audience" (IV.i.76) to Henry. Falstaff generally finds a less receptive audience than in *1H4*. He entreats Quickly, for instance, with "Dost thou hear, hostess?" and "Dost thou hear?" only to be told "Tilly-fally, Sir John, ne'er tell me" (II.iv.77,80–81). Thus newly isolated, he addresses people who have just gone out of

earshot (I.ii.239, IV.iii.84–85) and, as if in desperation, seems to
address the play's audience more than before in his
soliloquies.[18]

Finally, the topic of deafness colors the relations between Hal
and the Lord Chief Justice in a special way. In the story as
received by Shakespeare, one of the salient facts about the
LCJ was Hal's having assaulted him.[19] Shakespeare, by not
dramatizing the incident, remarkably deemphasizes it—probably, as Humphreys suggests,[20] because it would be overly
damaging to Hal if shown. But the assault is referred to, on three
occasions.[21] And, interestingly, among the several available versions of the incident, Shakespeare actually chooses the one
which seems *most* damaging to Hal, when he has Falstaff taunt
the justice

> For the box of the ear that the Prince gave you, he gave
> it like a rude prince, and you took it like a sensible lord
> (I.ii.193–95)

as if this detail were thematically too germane to be omitted,
even though it less befits Hal than the madcap prince imagined
by characters in the tetralogy. And in any case, Hal atones when
as Henry V he confirms the LCJ, telling him "My voice shall
sound as you do prompt mine ear" (V.ii.119).

4. *"I, from the Orient to the drooping West,*
   Making the wind my post-horse, still unfold
   The acts commenced on this ball of earth."

As we have seen, the unfolding of acts—narration or reporting of acts past, present, and future—is a significant and prevalent kind of speech action in *2H4*. When Rumour talks simply of
"reports" he emphasizes certain features of the act, such as
truth-value and transmission from tongue to tongue, which
place reporting in the context of other speech acts which may or
may not possess these features. But when he speaks of "unfold-

[18]He addresses the play's audience directly, as "you," at V.i.81–82; see also
III.ii.319 and IV.iii.101, where second person pronouns in Falstaff's soliloquy,
though not definitely manifesting it, do suggest address to the play's audience.
[19]For a description of the versions of the story and the sources, see Humphreys, "Introduction," pp. xxix–xliii.
[20]*Ibid.* p. xxxix.
[21]I.ii.55–56, I.ii. 193–95, and V.ii.80.

ing acts" he emphasizes the propositional content—the acts narrated. So seen, narration or reportage becomes an important example of the relation between (1) *"action"* and (2) *language* or *speech* as conceived of in the play.

On the surface, at least, narration suggests a fairly simple and clear opposition between action (what is narrated) on the one hand and language or speech (the narration itself) on the other. This conceptual dichotomy seems to obtain in most of the play's references to reporting or narration. Occasionally, though, even in a reference to narration the matter is less simple. For instance, when Northumberland imagines Morton, who is about to report the battle of Shrewsbury,

> Stopping my greedy ear with their bold deeds:
> But in the end, to stop my ear indeed,
> Thou hast a sigh to blow away this praise
>
> (I.i.78–80)

the clarity of the speech-vs.-action dichotomy is threatened first by the substitution of "deeds" for "narration of deeds," and then further by "indeed." A different complication appears in Henry's

> all my reign hath been but as a scene
> Acting that argument
>
> (IV.v.197–98)

where we have a kind of mirror image of narration, with action matching or fitting itself to a "story" rather than vice versa.

These references to reporting or narration comprise a major locus of the relation between speech and action as a dichotomy, but we find the same conception elsewhere. It is part of the naivete of Mrs. Quickly's carefully circumstantial accounts, her telling precisely what was being *done* when such-and-such a thing was *said*. In

> For that same word 'rebellion' did divide
> The action of their bodies from their souls
>
> (I.i.194–95)

the dichotomy appears as a confused antagonism. It appears frequently in discussion of battle, usually voiced by or associated with the rebel party, as above, or as when they are accused of "turning the word to sword" (IV.ii.10), or when they speak of the danger of "Using the names of men instead of men" (I.iii.57). This last, however, is echoed by Westmoreland in "Our battle is more full of names than yours" (IV.i.154)—a boast that, incidentally, rings slightly hollow inasmuch as some of those names, we have just learned, are Wart, Shadow, and Feeble.

The same dichotomy seems involved in Westmoreland's

> Wherefore do you so ill translate yourself
> Out of the speech of peace that bears such grace
> Into the harsh and boist'rous tongue of war . . . ?
> (IV.i.47–49)

though it is difficult here to put one's finger on just how the relation between "action" and "speech" is being conceived of. As suggested above (p. 90), the passage seems clearly metaphorical, with "speech" or "tongue" standing for action in general. The metaphor, as I have tried to show, serves to generalize the theme of the proliferated tongues, but here the use of it (rather than, say, metonomy) implies that "speech" and "action" are dichotomous or at least distinctly separate conceptual entities. Yet the metaphor, built on the dichotomy, is in fact a figurative denial of the dichotomy; is, in other words, a claim that "action is speech." Through this figurative denial the metaphor lays the ground for a different conception of the relation between "speech" and "action." For instance, if we reverse the metaphor we have "speech is action," a claim that need not be at all figurative.

This latter conception of speech as action appears occasionally in the play. It underlies Falstaff's

> Nay, and a do nothing but speak nothing, a shall be
> nothing here
> (II.iv.189–90)

and also the several mentions of legal (and thus verbal) "actions."

As regards the relation between "speech" and "action," all these passages are conceptually simple compared to what Henry says in his last important speech to Hal:

> Be it thy course to busy giddy minds
> With foreign quarrels, that action hence borne out

2 Henry IV 113

> May waste the memory of the former days.
> More would I, but my lungs are wasted so
> That strength of speech is utterly denied me.
> (IV.v.213–17)

The repeated "waste[d]" and the chiming "out"-"utterly" insist on as much as they vex a parallelism and equation between action borne out of the realm and speech borne out of the king's body. But the parataxis here seems to make it finally impossible to determine whether the equation is of the form "action is speech," or some other.

Thus far we have examined variations on two basic conceptual models—the first, and more frequently exemplified, being the speech-vs.-action dichotomy, and the second being the idea of speech as a kind of action. In our examples of the second model, the specific kind of speech action at issue is Austin's "locutionary act," the act of uttering or saying such-and-such a thing. That speech action should be so conceived is in keeping with the play's general retrenchment and limiting of attention to mere locution and mere words. However on at least one occasion we find a more subtle and sophisticated model. It is of course Hal who implies this when he instructs the Lord Chief Justice

> Be it your charge, my lord,
> To see perform'd the tenor of my word.
> (V.v.70–71)

Here the addition of the term "tenor" to mediate between "performance" or "action" and "word" or utterance takes us quite beyond the conceptual models prevalent elsewhere in the play. In passing, as it were, Hal once again shows that he sees through the surface of language to comparatively profound considerations of speech action.

Conclusion

In *2H4* Henry Bolingbroke, who ascended the throne as a "silent king," comes to the silence of death, now wishing to speak more:

> More would I, but my lungs are wasted so
> That strength of speech is utterly denied me.
> (IV.v.216–17)

The world of conceptions and uses of language that he had precipitated in *R2* and reigned over in *1H4* here dies with him. The act of silence had proved viable in opposition to Richard's absolutist tongue, but in *2H4* "and a do nothing but speak nothing, a shall be nothing here." Generally here, I think, we find a linguistic world antithetical to Richard's, one which was viable in opposition to Richard's (and then to Hotspur's) "one tongue," declining because, now prevailing, it runs to extremes and excesses as vicious and therefore self-destructive in their way as Richard's.

"How ill it follows," says Poins to Hal, "after you have laboured so hard, you should talk so idly!" (II.ii.28–29). But in this world *"full of tongues"* all talk is more or less idle. Verbal interaction, vitiated by deafness and idiolect, becomes inconsequential and tends toward mere activity. With each tongue its own authority, true and false tidings, rumors, slanders, reminiscences, and prophecies wander unchecked. The destruction of Richard's vain timelessness, which gave birth to the "justling time" of vigorous decisive action in *1H4*, now results in a world where all are "time's subjects." Consciousness of time—of its effects of aging, illness, and death in the individual and of the random events brought by "the revolution of the times" in the state—seems to obviate heroism, so that at Gaultree battle is forestalled and loss of life prevented by a "mis-taken" word. Mistaking is endemic, and attempts at making more than token sense of verbal intercourse are rare. Mowbray, attempting it, says "But he hath forc'd us to compel this offer" (IV.i.147) and approaches nonsense. More typical is Shallow's less ambitious analysis:

> Give me pardon, sir; if, sir; you come with news from
> the court, I take it there's but two ways, either to utter
> them or conceal them.
>
> (V.iii.106–8)

A lowering of sights to the mere word or mere locution is shown by the extensiveness of quotation.

Thus Henry's sons John, Clarence, and Gloucester in a sense represent the entire realm when, after their father's death, they meet "like men that had forgot to speak" (V.ii.22). Hal, how-

ever, is not included in this "we." The times are such that he too
suffers a "heavy descension" (II.ii.166)—from his hard labors at
Shrewsbury to weariness and idle talk. Yet, as he says, "in everything the purpose must weigh with the folly" (II.ii.168–
69) and, if he does not have occasion to make such emphatic
promises as before, he continues quite as purposive, studying
his companions "like a strange tongue," looking upon and learning the prevailing "gross terms" which he will, "in the perfect-
ness of time, / Cast off" (Iv.iv.71–75). Listening in a world of
deafness, becoming polyglot in a world of tongues tending
toward idiolect, he bides his time until he ascends the throne
to establish a reign of new conceptions and uses of language.
The speech action of Henry V in the last act of *2H4* is more authoritative and consequential than any to be found earlier in the
play—perhaps than any found earlier in the tetralogy—and
what he says about language shows none of the reductiveness
that has recently prevailed.

How well his long preparation has served him, how little he
has shared the linguistic vitiation, and what a distinct change he
thus brings, is apparent when, to those who "meet like men that
had forgot to speak," he announces

> Now call we our high court of parliament.
> (V.ii.134)

The point is important enough to be made again at the end of
the play, when John says "The King hath call'd his parliament"
(V.v.103). For Hal has learned, not forgotten, how to speak.
After Richard's overweening univocal absolutism, after Henry
IV's silence and reticence, we have a many-tongued monarch
who, using a wide range of language purposefully and responsibly, initiates a reign of "high . . . parliament."

CHAPTER FOUR

❧ *Henry V*

Critical commentary on *Henry V* is thinner and more divided than writing on the other Lancastrian plays.[1] It concerns itself mostly with two large topics: questions about the moral-ethical-political system presented, and the "genre" question of just what sort of play it is. With both topics (they are related, of course) the critical division is understandable, and with both it results from Shakespeare's having carried out in *H5* atypical procedures, procedures which in fact are unique in the canon: the use of an eminently successful military figure as hero, and the use of a chorus as a framing device. The canon thus provides less support for the interpretation of *H5* than for Shakespeare's other plays. The polarization and disarray of the commentary, if nothing else, shows that *H5* is certainly a "problem play" (perhaps even a "problem comedy") but, whereas one can invoke *Troilus and Cressida* and *Measure for Measure* in dealing with *All's Well that Ends Well*, *H5* perplexes in solitude.

The discussion below bears on the traditional areas of concern of the commentary in ways which I will try to suggest. But my

[1] A responsible survey of the criticism of *H5* is provided by Ronald Berman, *A Reader's Guide to Shakespeare's Plays*, pp. 65–70. Berman, who has himself written on the play, finds that "There are essentially three groups of critics: those who hate the play and its hero; those who admire both; those who attempt to remain neutral" (p. 66), thus giving a good sense of the division and comparative thinness of the play's criticism. See also Paul Jorgensen, "Accidental Judgements, Casual Slaughters and Purposes Mistook."

primary focus is, again, on the subject of language. It has largely
been ignored in the criticism of *H5*,[2] in spite of the fact the topic
figures as prominently here as in the preceding plays. And, with
the rest of the tetralogy and the preceding discussion of it as a
context, it provides a viewpoint from which one can see that *H5*,
however peculiar, is more deeply unified and comprehensible
than a survey of the criticism might lead one to believe.

The chapter has five main sections. The first two deal with the
most important thematic and dramaturgical matters, the Babel
theme of the variety of languages (I) and the messages (II); the
second two concern the two most prominent speakers, the
Chorus (III) and Henry (IV); and the last (V) is a summary
conclusion.

I

In *H5* the reality which the Babel story attempts to explain, rationalize, or justify—the fact of the variety of languages—is given much greater emphasis and is dramatized
much more extensively than in the preceding plays of the tetralogy. The main example of this variety is the use of French, and
in large sections of three scenes, comprising almost one-tenth of
the text, we observe various characters confronting the French-
English language barrier.

In the first of these, III.iv, the French princess Katherine
learns some English words from her lady-in-waiting, Alice.
Though the English words—"hand," "arm," "elbow," and so
on—are mentioned, the dialogue is entirely in French; this is the
only scene in a foreign language that Shakespeare wrote. What
happens is the language lesson, simply that. There is perhaps a
slight characterization of Katherine in ways not directly relevant
to this study, but virtually all of what Shakespeare has chosen to
show concerns language.

The scene immediately follows that of Henry's first victory in
France, so that there is a kind of irony in Katherine's beginning

[2]Although the characteristic language of the minor characters has received
some attention. See, for example, John W. Draper, "The Humor of Corporal
Nym," and the essay on "Ancient Pistol" in Leslie Hotson, *Shakespeare's Sonnets
Dated.*

> Alice, tu as été en Angleterre, et tu parles bien le
> langage
>
> (III.iv.1–2)

and continuing

> Je te prie, m'enseignez; il faut que j'apprenne à parler
> (ll. 4–5)

The lesson proceeds, and Alice's exclamations of approval—
"il est fort bon Anglais" (ll. 20–21), "Excellent, Madame!"
(l. 61)—contribute to Katherine's optimism. Throughout there
is a sweet pastoral feeling which derives not only from the inno-
cence of a princess's learning a language (in contrast to Henry's
horrifying description of war in the preceding scene) but also
from the simplicity of her conception of language. Her pride is
childlike because learning a few "mots d'Anglais" is a farther cry
than she realizes from learning English. Her achievement is
further limited by the fact that all her "mots" are nouns. That
they are almost all names for parts of the body adds to the
childlike quality of the lesson and also prepares the ground for
Katherine's becoming a figure of what is natural, fertile, sexual.
But for all her naivete, Katherine is shown in the scene as being like her future husband in that when she talks about language, she talks about the practical matter of translation from
one tongue to another and shows ambition for becoming
multilingual.

The second French-English scene is Pistol's capture of a
French soldier during the battle of Agincourt (IV.iv). At first they
are unable to cross the language barrier:

> *Pistol.* Yield, cur!
> *French Soldier.* Je pense que vous êtes le gentil-homme
>   de bonne qualité.
> *Pist.* Qualitie calmie custure me! Art thou a gentleman?
>   What is thy name? Discuss.
> *Fr. Sol.* O seigneur Dieu!
> *Pist.* O, Signieur Dew should be a gentleman: Perpend
>   my words, O signieur Dew, and mark
>
> (IV.iv.1–8)

until the Boy serves as interpreter. Most of his translations are
very close, but some are rather free, and the question of the

freedom of his translation is of interest particularly because, while he is the tetralogy's most proficient translator, he himself may at one point (when he translates "très distingué" as "thrice worthy") founder on the fact that (as Katherine says later) "les langues des hommes sont pleines de tromperies"—depending on whether we take his translations as literal or free.

Before leaving this scene it is worth dwelling a little more on this Boy, because his career in the last two plays of the tetralogy is interesting and has not usually received much comment. In *2H4* we see him as Falstaff's page, provided by Hal; it is he who serves as Falstaff's spokesman in the beginning of his first encounter with the Lord Chief Justice. There, and in many of his other appearances, the Boy is reticent and obedient; but there are other moments when he shows himself witty, discerning, and rather cynical about Falstaff & Co. Early in *H5* it is the Boy who announces Falstaff's illness to Bardolph, Nym, Pistol, and Quickly; and later he and Quickly describe Falstaff's death. Then we see the Boy in the company of Nym, Bardolph, and Pistol. After Fluellen has driven them from the stage, the Boy remains to comment in soliloquy on their pretended valor and real cowardice. At the end of this long soliloquy he resolves

> I must leave them, and seek some better service: their villany goes against my weak stomach, and therefore I must cast it up.
>
> (III.ii.54–56)

But when we next see him he is still with Pistol, in the translation scene mentioned above. At the end of this scene, when Pistol and his prisoner have left the stage, the Boy remains to speak, again in soliloquy, his last words in the tetralogy:

> I must stay with the lackeys, with the luggage of our camp: the French might have a good prey of us if he knew of it; for there is none to guard it but boys.
>
> (IV.iv.76–80)

We soon learn that the French have indeed had "a good prey" of him:

> *Fluellen.* Kill the poys and the luggage! 'tis expressly against the law of arms: 'tis as arrant a piece of knavery, mark you now, as can be offer't; in your conscience now, is it not?

> *Gower.* 'Tis certain there's not a boy left alive; and the
> cowardly rascals that ran from the battle ha' done
> this slaughter.
>
> (IV.viii.1–7)

The fact that this particular boy has been killed is left for us to
deduce and consider, since he is not mentioned specifically here
or later; and yet the grounds for the deduction are made very
plain.

All this is curious, interesting and, I would maintain, significant. And it seems to me that much of the significance of the
Boy's career lies in his being a sort of double, substitute, alter
ego, or poetic representative of Hal. That is, the Boy is that part
of Hal which remains with the Boar's Head crew even after Hal
has separated himself from them. (To say this is to deal in illogic,
or the logic of dream and myth, which seems to violate a basic
principle of this study, namely, the principle of the distinction
and integrity of dramatic characters. However, fictions often
operate by the logic of dream and myth; apparent and partial
violation of the principle of integrity of dramatic characters may
serve to throw that principle into stronger relief; and in the case
in point, following the dream logic brings us back to questions of
language, the main concern of the study.)

Among the pieces of evidence for taking the Boy as a part of
Hal left with the Boar's Head crew are Hal's having assigned the
Boy to Falstaff; the fact that Hal and the Boy never appear together in *H5* (and only once, briefly, in *2H4*, where the Boy's role
is, as it were, announced); the Boy's similarity to Hal in knowing
the whole crew and being willing to uphold a while the humor
of their idleness; and the fact that in *H5* he and Hal are the only
characters with the autonomy of soliloquy. Finally, there is the
fact that, upon hearing that the French have killed the boys in
the camp, Hal says "I was not angry since I came to France /
Until this instant" and (according to Gower) retaliates with what
critics have found his most reprehensible action, ordering the
killing of the French prisoners. Hal's seemingly excessive anger,
according to my interpretation, is directed at having been surprised, for the only time in the tetralogy, by the exigencies of the
role of king. He was able to reject Falstaff partly, perhaps, because he left a part of himself with Falstaff. But he is angry and

surprised when the great public action he undertakes as king results in the death of this part of himself. Or, to put the matter another way, Hal's accession involves rejecting not only Falstaff but also his former self; and if Falstaff dies, so does his young companion in the person of the Boy, at the hands of those over whom King Henry V triumphs.[3]

Viewing the role of the Boy in this way not only seems to clarify such things in the play as Hal's apparently excessive anger at the killing of the boys by the French; in particular, it also allows us to take more seriously than we otherwise might the Boy's numerous remarks about language, for they thus reflect something of Hal with his authority. What the Boy seems most to reflect is Hal's facility with various tongues. But the Boy is also like Hal in seeing through Pistol, Bardolph, and Nym; and he expresses his knowledge of them repeatedly by talking about their speech action:

> For Pistol, he hath a killing tongue and a quiet sword;
> by the means whereof a' breaks words, and keeps
> whole weapons. For Nym, he hath heard that men of
> few words are the best men; and therefore he scorns to
> say his prayers, lest a' should be thought a coward: but
> his few bad words are matched with as few good
> deeds.

> (III.ii.34–41)

There is a kind of cynicism, disillusionment, or suspicion about language here; but it is very different from the cynicism of Falstaff's speech about honor. While Falstaff is cynical about language itself or, specifically, about words themselves, the Boy is cynical about ways language is used. Admittedly risking

[3]In *Shakespeare's Histories at Stratford, 1951* by J. Dover Wilson and T. C. Worsley there is a photograph (between pp. 74–75) of the production of *H5* showing Fluellen presenting the body of the Boy to Henry, who, according to the caption, is saying "I was not angry since I came to France / Until this instant" (IV.vii.57–58). Though there is no textual authority for this stage business, it suggests that the part of the Boy was interpreted in ways similar to mine; and the fact that one of the few photographs of the production shows this moment suggests that Wilson and Worsley took that interpretation very seriously. Nevertheless, considered evaluation of this character is evanescent: in the cast of characters Wilson and Worsley provide, he disappears among "Ladies-in-Waiting, Soldiers, Sailors, Citizens, Servants" (p. 96).

exaggeration, one might say that Falstaff is theoretical, abstract, absolutist, and medieval in reducing the very institution of language to "air," and the Boy is pragmatic, particular, relativist, and Renaissance in focusing his attention on the uses and misuses of that institution.

In these respects the Boy seems to exhibit a part of an attitude to language which we may attribute to Hal. The Boy's recognition of improper uses of language seems indeed a negative correlate of the recognition of proper uses of language, one that Hal himself exhibits in numerous ways throughout the play.

The third French-English scene is Hal's courtship of Katherine, V.ii. Katherine in her first speech raises the problem of tongues:

> Your majesty shall mock at me; I cannot speak your
> England.
>
> (ll. 102–3)

(She has, however, learned a great deal of English since her lesson with Alice.) In Henry's reply,

> . . . if you will love me soundly with your French
> heart, I will be glad to hear you confess it brokenly
> with your English tongue.
>
> (ll. 104–6)

the ambiguity of "tongue" which, threatening to collapse, was a symptom of the malaise of *2H4*, is matter for assured play. This bodes well; it establishes a mood of comic transcendence for the encounter which is the most intensive proving of Hal's polyglotism.

Throughout the scene the problem of the proliferated tongues is present and recognized; it arises again almost immediately when Hal continues "Do you like me, Kate?" and she says "Pardonnez-moi, I cannot tell wat is 'like me!'" (ll. 107–8).[4] But here again her statement and exemplification of the difficulty is more matter for Hal's play: "An angel is like you, Kate, and you are like an angel" (ll. 109–10). The lady-in-waiting,

---

[4]Katherine's "Pardonnez-moi" echoes the Duke of York's "Speak it in French, king, say 'pardonne moy'" in *R2* (V.iii.117), which is Shakespeare's first example in the tetralogy of the difficulty occasioned by language barriers.

Alice, is present to translate occasionally, but she is not much needed, apparently having proved a good teacher. Hal, like Katherine, can cross the language barrier. And though he woos in "fausse French" and she replies in "broken English," the repeated emphasis on the difficulty makes all the more impressive their ease in overcoming it, communicating to the point of betrothal.[5]

While the three French-English scenes alone would suffice to establish variety of languages as a theme of major importance in the play, it also appears often elsewhere, importantly in the Irish, Welsh, and Scottish dialects of Macmorris, Fluellen, and Jamy, and also incidentally, for example, in Pistol's occasional French tags. Thus the idea of proliferated tongues, having been significant through the three earlier plays, pervades *H5*. And here the idea is given not only greater emphasis but also a different kind of emphasis. Without exception, I believe, the moments and scenes having to do with the variety of languages are, like Hal's courtship of Katherine, comic. A good index of the distance traversed by the tetralogy is a comparison of the relaxed genial comedy of Hal's and Katherine's courtship with Mowbray's lament at having been banished to France in the beginning of *R2*:

> And now my tongue's use is to me no more
> Than an unstringed viol or a harp,
> Or like a cunning instrument cased up.
>   (*R2*, I.iii.161–63)

What has immediately happened is the accession of Hal, the responsible polyglot, of whom Canterbury in this play says

> Hear him but reason in divinity,
> And, all-admiring, with an inward wish
> You would desire the king were made a prelate:
> Hear him debate of commonwealth affairs,
> You would say it hath been all in all his study:
> List his discourse of war, and you shall hear
> A fearful battle render'd you in music:
> Turn him to any cause of policy,

[5]This scene is discussed here only briefly because we shall return to it below.

> The Gordian knot of it he will unloose,
> Familiar as his garter; that, when he speaks,
> The air, a charter'd libertine, is still,
> And the mute wonder lurketh in men's ears,
> To steal his sweet and honey'd sentences.
>
> (I.i.38–50)

The consequences of the fall of the tower of Babel have been not only faced and recognized, as in the *H4* plays, but also turned to good account and so overcome that the fall of the tower seems fortunate. The proliferated tongues which most recently in *2H4* had resulted in a world of deafness and idiolect are here ordered into a harmony that depends on translation and willingness to communicate and hear.

The Dauphin, in fact, may say more than he means in his lines

> And let us do it with no show of fear;
> No, with no more than if we heard that England
> Were busied with a Whitsun morris-dance.
>
> (II.iv.23–25)

For *H5* does enact something analogous to the miracle of Whit-sunday or Pentecost, when the proliferation of tongues was transcended. The play is full of images of harmony, unity-in-variety; and it is within an order like that of "broken music," or "many arrows loosed several ways" which "Come to one mark," that the proliferation of tongues is transcended here. It is an order that involves and recognizes the variety of tongues rather than one like Richard's which seems to deny that variety: even the miracle of Pentecost involved speaking in tongues and thus did not obliterate the effects of the fall of the tower.

The last act of the play shows this sort of transcendence not only very extensively in Hal's courtship and betrothal but also momentarily in that act's other principal event, the treaty, the only stated articles of which are the marriage and the demand that the French king, writing Hal, shall address him

> In French, Notre très-cher filz Henry, Roy d'Angleterre,
> Héritier de France; and thus in Latin, Praeclarissimus
> filius noster Henricus, Rex Angliae, et Haeres Franciae.
>
> (V.ii.357–60)

And then, almost at the end of the act, when Queen Isabel says

> So be there 'twixt your kingdoms such a spousal
> ·
> That English may as French, French Englishmen,
> Receive each other! God speak this Amen!
> (V.ii.380–86)

the harmony of tongues is measured against and legitimized by
the only tongue which can be absolute.[6]

II

In each of the French-English scenes discussed above
there are translators (the Boy and Alice) whose position is
formally much like that of a messenger—only they carry messages across a language barrier, rather than traverse spatial distance. Thus in the translation we find two major subjects of
the play overlapping: proliferated tongues, and messages and
messengers.[7]

Sending and delivering messages is perhaps the most talked
about as well as one of the most frequently and conspicuously
performed speech acts in *H5*. Most of the messages are exchanged between the French and English courts. In the fifth act,

[6]Before leaving the topic of the variety of tongues, I would mention an odd
feature of the play which has received little if any comment: there are scenes in
the French court and camp in which everyone speaks English. Probably critics
have not found this worthy of note because the convention involved (call it that
of translation) is so common, being practically necessary in all fictions set in
language communities other than that of the audience. Shakespeare himself
relies on it in many of his plays and in his narrative poems, and in most of them
it does not deserve special attention. But surely in *H5*, of all Shakespeare's plays,
it does: because of the Chorus's rather unusual emphasis on other conventions
of the fiction and his requests that the audience recognize and accept them;
because of the general thematic importance, within the play, of the fact of the
variety of languages; and, most obviously, because side by side with the French
scenes in English we also have French scenes in French. Thus it would seem that
this normally insignificant convention must be significant here, perhaps in part
because it enables Shakespeare to produce *in the audience* something like the
miracle of Pentecost. The speech of the Frenchmen has become as their own,
completely intelligible.

[7]The treaty in V.ii, which codifies bilingual vocatives for letters from the
French king to Henry, is another example of the overlap of the Babel theme and
the topic of messages. It should be noted that sending and delivering messages
are "speech acts" by my extension of Austin's and Searle's uses of the term.

with the courts "face to face and royal eye to eye" (V.ii.30), there is no need for messengers; but for the first four acts there is an elaborate and orderly sequence of messages. It comprises a considerable portion of the play and, if only for that reason, deserves comment.

The emphasis on the orderly transference of information by messages serves to distinguish the verbal action of *H5*—Hal's linguistic world—from the domain of Rumour in *2H4*. But there is more to the matter, and it can perhaps best be brought out by comparing communication via messenger with the norm of direct communication, thus examining the effect of the abnormal case's relative prevalence in the play.

First, communication by message would seem to contribute to the often noted epic quality of the play, because it amounts to an enlargement of the verbal action. In direct communication, with the continual possibility of immediate reply, things can be (and, in this part of Shakespeare's career, increasingly are) worked out through a complex and subtle interplay consisting of many brief, small verbal acts. But via messenger such interplay becomes impractical. Verbal action by messenger is thus naturally larger than life—larger than the norm of direct verbal action. To make ample use of the occasion the sender makes his speech acts unusually clear, explicit, and perfected; he can do so because he has time to consider the message before sending it, and because there is no possibility of his being interrupted before the action is completed. Therefore the messages sent from one court to the other in *H5* are unusually large—long, clear, and completed—verbal acts. It would of course be possible for a writer to provide this sort of verbal action for characters speaking directly to each other; and in epic this happens. In *H5*, however, direct interaction is much more lively and lifelike than the sequence of messages.

There are other reasons for the prominence of messages in the play which have less to do with its epic quality and more to do with the immediate concerns of this study. We have noted in earlier chapters the peculiarly undirected nature of Richard's speech, the end of its sway, and the movement of the tetralogy into a realm of verbal action in which direction of address is increasingly important. The messages in *H5* are virtually emblematic of this change, which is completed in the play. For a message by definition is sent *to* someone, has a direction. The very concept of message involves not only essential but also explicit reference to the speaker-hearer axis. (Nor is it odd that this relation should be so emphasized just where it does not obviously obtain: in fact it does obtain *even then* — communication can take place even when speaker and hearer are not in one another's presence.)

What the messages make explicit is generally characteristic of the verbal action of this play, which itself is messagelike inasmuch as its direction of address is clear; people speak *to* each other. And, since they also hear each other, the action is interaction. The hindrances to interaction are external and accidental, such as distance or language barriers, rather than, as often before, characteristic ways of conceiving and using language and characteristic deformations of the speech-situation. [8]

But while interaction via messenger differs from the norm of direct interaction in some respects, in most the two are alike. In particular, features of the illocutionary act like those we have noted in analysis of direct interaction in preceding chapters are also present in messages: the sequence of royal messages constitutes a verbal agon like those we have considered before. It is to this agon, larger and more extensive than any other in the play, that we now turn.

There are four interchanges in this agon of messages. The first is the occasion of the gift of the tennis balls, I.ii. Almost from the beginning of the scene we know of the impending interchange:

> *Westmoreland.* Shall we call in th' ambassador, my
>   liege?
> *King Henry.* Not yet, my cousin: we would be resolv'd,
>   Before we hear him, of some things of weight
>   That task our thoughts, concerning us and France.
>   (I.ii.3–6)

[8]Pistol's fustian is a relic of wilfully noncommunicative speech, and even his eccentricity can partly be overcome:

> *Fluellen.* Aunchient Pistol, I do partly understand your meaning.
> *Pistol.* Why then, rejoice therefore.
>   (III.vi.51–53)

Thus the ensuing long discussion of the propriety of Henry's claim to France and the feasibility of enforcing it serves once and for all in the play to show the grave and complex preparation presupposed for engagement in the agon. Arguments are presented to Henry; he asks a question, raises a possible objection, but for the most part is a silent auditor until his "Call in the messengers sent from the Dauphin" (l. 221) signals what he next announces: "now are we well resolv'd" (l. 222). The momentary suspense here of the court's knowing that he is resolved without yet knowing what his resolution is contributes to our sense of Henry's authority.

The ambassador's initial question,

> May't please your majesty to give us leave
> Freely to render what we have in charge;
> Or shall we sparingly show you far off
> The Dauphin's meaning and our embassy?
> (ll. 227–40)

raises the specter of the wilful deafness that had loomed large in *2H4*. But Henry's reply

> with frank and with uncurbed plainness
> Tell us the Dauphin's mind
> (ll. 244–45)

dismisses the possibility and so takes leave of the linguistic world of the preceding play. The interaction then begins.

It is initiated by the Dauphin's insulting and therefore provocative message. Such an opening gives the entire succeeding action the semblance of a working through of the French error's consequences, thus according a kind of moral endorsement to the English. Yet Shakespeare does not present Henry merely as reacting. He has already resolved

> France being ours, we'll bend it to our awe
> Or break it all to pieces.
> (ll. 224–25)

Furthermore, though the Dauphin's message is the first dramatized action in the series, the message itself, according to the ambassador, is "in answer" to Henry's "sending into France" claiming "certain dukedoms" (ll. 246–49).

The fact that Henry's interlocutor here is the Dauphin rather
than the French king is given an emphasis which contributes to
our sense of the French contempt for Henry. It also begins the
characterization of the Dauphin as impetuous and foolhardy—
something of a French Hotspur—and of his father as reticent,
cautious, slow to move— something of a French Henry IV. Finally, the identity of Henry's interlocutor is emphasized here
because in the succeeding action he has a significantly changing
series of interlocutors, each being France's spokesman in turn.

We are not shown the French ambassadors' delivery of
Henry's long reply

> We are glad the Dauphin is so pleasant with us
> ·
> Tell you the Dauphin I am coming on,
> To venge me as I may and to put forth
> My rightful hand in a well-hallow'd cause.
> So get you hence in peace; and tell the Dauphin
> His jest will savour but of shallow wit
> When thousands weep more than did laugh at it
> (ll. 259–96)

but we hear from the constable that they have returned not only
with that message but also with descriptions of

> With what great state he [Henry] heard their embassy,
> How well supplied with noble counsellors,
> How modest in exception, and withal
> How terrible in constant resolution.
> (II.iv.32–35)

Therefore the first interchange is complete: France has spoken,
England has spoken, each has heard.

Were this a normal, evenly matched, continuing verbal interaction, France would speak next. But at this juncture we hear
nothing of a message to England. What happens, rather, is that
England speaks again. Henry's aggressive initiative in the verbal
intercourse reflects his coming "with full power" (II.iv.1) into
France. The timing of the arrival of Henry's word—just as the
French king is admonishing the Dauphin

> Think we King Harry strong
> ·

> . . . and let us fear
> The native mightiness and fate of him
>   (II.iv.48–64)

—makes Henry's usurpation of France's turn in the conversation especially portentous.

Compared to the earlier French messenger, Exeter in his delivery of Henry's message is bold and direct. The first part is to the king, and he comes brusquely to the point:

> *French King.*   From our brother of England?
> *Exeter.* From him; and thus he greets your majesty.
> He wills you, in the name of God Almighty
> That you divest yourself.
>   (II.iv.75–78)

Exeter's authoritative manner has a complex effect. In a sense it shows him a more perfect medium than the French ambassador, for he can transmit not only the message but also its manner and tone. It means that we have a greater sense of an action's being transmitted. And since thus we have a greater sense of Henry's presence, his manner suggests that the English nation is a more unified body than the French.

These effects are heightened by the fact that when Exeter has stated Henry's claim and bidding and has apparently finished his message the French king can question him further:

> *French King.* Or what else follows?
> *Exeter.* Bloody constraint.
>   (ll. 96–97)

This interchange formally distinguishes Exeter's status as messenger from that of the French ambassador, with whom there was no interlocution, in the delivery of the message, so that he might as well have handed Henry a letter from the Dauphin.

One is accustomed to think that the familiar forms of direct and indirect quotation exhaust the possibilities of transmitting messages. The format of Exeter's speeches, however, belies those simplistic categories. There is a kind of indirect quotation—

> he bids you then resign
> Your crown and kingdom
>   (ll. 93–94)

but here the present tense of the verb naming Henry's speech act does not fit familiar categories. We are farther from familiar categories in Exeter's

> He wills you . . .
> That you divest yourself. . . .
>
> (ll. 77–78)

For here we have a "message-radical" or "proposition-radical"—*(that) you divest*—as in indirect quotation, but "wills" does *not* name a speech act. And we are farthest from familiar categories of message-transmission in moments like

> Therefore in fierce tempest is he coming,
> In thunder and in earthquake like a Jove
>
> (ll. 99–100)

where there is a message-radical *tout court,* bare of any frame referring to Henry as the sender.

   Having delivered his message to the king, Exeter concludes

> This is his claim, his threat'ning, and my message
>
> (l. 110)

laying open some of the complexity of his status as messenger; and the king states that he will reply "To-morrow."
   The second part of Exeter's message is for the Dauphin, "To whom expressly I bring greeting too" (l. 112).[9] It is in two parts, the first—

> Scorn and defiance; slight regard, contempt,
> And anything that may not misbecome
> The mighty sender, doth he prize you at
>
> (ll. 117–19)

—a sort of formal insulting, and the second a hypothetical warning of woe to France in default of the king's granting Henry's demands—

> He'll call you to so hot an answer . . .
> That caves and womby vaultages of France

---

[9]The "expressly" bifurcated direction of address is, at a distance, characteristic of the "mighty sender" of the message, Hal.

> Shall chide your trespass and return your mock
> In second accent of his ordinance
>
> (ll. 123–26)

notably couched in metaphors of speech arts.

When the Dauphin replies with a message for Henry, Exeter takes the initiative of delivering his own warning that the Dauphin's estimate of Henry is mistaken. The king repeats that he will reply on the morrow, and there is a flourish signalling that the interview is concluded. But Exeter boldly continues it:

> Dispatch us with all speed, lest our king
> Come here himself to question our delay;
> For he is footed in this land already.
>
> (ll. 141–43)

The cautious French king will not be hurried:

> A night is but small breath and little pause
> To answer matters of this consequence.
>
> (ll. 145–46)

Thus incomplete, the second interchange ends.

We may assume Exeter's delivery of the French replies. Yet, in the ensuing excitement of Harfleur, there is no mention of it, so that we have no inkling of the substance of the French king's cautiously postponed reply. In a sense, then, this reply of his does not exist, or, better, it is postponed past the "small breath and little pause" he demands, past Harfleur, and is in fact the message he sends to Henry to begin the third interchange of the royal agon.

This interchange is presented more fully than the others in that before it occurs we see the French message dispatched in the French court (III.vi). The king gives his message—"sharp defiance" (l. 37) and "that we send / To know what willing ransom he will give" (ll. 62–63)—to the Constable of France, who is to give it to Montjoy, who is to convey it to Henry. On the face of it, this relay team might seem a pointless detail. However, I think that part of its point is to show the French society, a chain of mechanical linkages, as a less perfect medium for the king's word than the English society, an organic whole.

In any case, the third interchange is also fuller than the others by virtue of its being the only complete interchange in which Henry's interlocutor is the French king. By now the Dauphin is out of his depth and cannot participate in the action he has rashly begun. That the king in a single speech—

> haste on Montjoy,
> And let him say to England that we send
> To know what willing ransom he will give.
> Prince Dauphin, you shall stay with us in Rouen
> (III.v.61–64)

—dispatches the message and restricts the Dauphin emphasizes the increased gravity of the message agon. (The Dauphin makes a last brief appearance at Agincourt—

> O perdurable shame! let's stab ourselves.
> Be these the wretches that we play'd at dice for?
> (IV.v.7–8)

—and then simply vanishes. There is no subsequent reference to him and, in the fifth act, when the two courts are together, it is as if he had never existed.)

In the following scene (III.vi), we have Montjoy's delivery of the message and Henry's reply. The French message is an interestingly expanded version of the one we saw the French king dispatch, as if Montjoy has had to articulate and formalize as well as transmit the action his master has at last been roused to perform. His opening

> Thus says my king: Say thou to Harry of England:
> Though we seemed dead, we did but sleep
> (III.vi.123–25)

with its rather superfluous second clause suggests that the message is being transmitted in an unwieldy and mechanical fashion.

The first part of the message is an overly insistent justification of the king's late entrance into the agon; and one of the figures of this justification— "now speak we on our cue" (l. 128)— amounts to an unwitting admission that the king's action is not self-determined. Still, in the second part of the message in which Henry is warned that he should be ransomed, the "voice," as Montjoy says, "is imperial" (l. 129), much more so than that in the Dauphin's messages.

Henry's long reply is in a "voice" or manner less "imperial" than this. He admits, "Though 'tis no wisdom to confess so much" (l .149), that his troops are

> with sickness much enfeebled,
> My numbers lessen'd. . . .
> (ll. 151–52)

Nevertheless, he will advance:

> The sum of all our answer is but this:
> We would not seek a battle as we are;
> Nor, as we are, we say we will not shun it:
> So tell your master.
> (ll. 169–72)

With this characteristic plain statement of intention, very different from both the French king's fulminations and the Dauphin's impertinence, the climactic third interchange ends.

The fourth (IV.iii) is basically a repetition of the third. Before the battle of Agincourt Montjoy appears at the English camp:

> Once again . . . to know of thee, King Harry,
> If for thy ransom thou wilt compound. . . .
> (IV.iii.79–80)

And Henry refuses:

> I pray thee, bear my former answer back:
> Bid them achieve me and then sell my bones.
> (IV.iii.90–91)

But an important difference between this and the preceding interchange is emphasized when, before answering, Henry asks "Who hath sent thee now?" (l. 88) and Montjoy replies "The Constable of France" (l. 89). The decline in the status of Henry's interlocutors suggests, I think, that the climax has been passed and foreshadows the outcome of the nonverbal action at Agincourt. And that the French at this juncture merely repeat their former question—"Will you be ransomed?"—also suggests decline (as did, for example, Falstaff's increasingly fatuous and helpless repetition in the *H4* plays).

The outcome of the battle of Agincourt is announced in a sort of denouement of the message agon, when Montjoy returns to admit the French defeat and to ask leave to bury the dead (IV.vii). This is the final and lowest stage in the shifting of Henry's French interlocutor—first the Dauphin, then the Dauphin and the king, then the king alone, then the decline to the Constable of France, and finally here the messenger himself, who speaks for the conquered nation.

In the sequence of royal messages we see, then, features of the local dramaturgy of speech action enlarged so that they become important features of the overall plot. Henry's usurping of the French turn in the interchange, for instance, is what we would term a bid for "control" of a verbal interaction. At the same time, the fact that this "conversation" is conducted by messenger make possible such complications as the changes in interlocutors in a two-party (France and England) interchange. And these complications are themselves significant: they contribute to "characteristic" differences between France and England.[10]

III

The speeches of the Chorus differ in kind from the speech action in earlier parts of the tetralogy being directed to the audience and in a realm of action quite distinct from the other action of the play. The speech of Rumour in *2H4* is similar; but the fact that the Chorus appears at intervals throughout *H5* distinguishes his speech and gives it a significance I shall try to assess.

[10]There are a few other messages outside the royal sequence, one of which is peculiar enough to deserve comment. This is Pistol's message to Fluellen,

> Tell him, I'll knock his leek about his pate
> Upon Saint Davy's day.
>
> (IV.i.54–55)

Pistol believes the messenger to be a gentleman volunteer soldier, but in fact it is Henry in disguise. Henry agrees to deliver the message. Later, however, we learn that the message has been delivered not by Henry but by Pistol himself. I confess that I do not quite see what to make of this, beyond taking it as an example of Henry's high-handed refusal to bind himself to the letter of the laws of verbal interaction.

As has often been noted, this Chorus, with his "invocation," "O, for a Muse of fire," his exalted language, wide-ranging and comprehensive descriptions of movements of armies, and so on, contributes to the epic quality of *H5*, so suited to the presentation of Henry as national martial hero. Although this quality is recognized by most of the play's recent commentators, it has proved controversial.[11] Many of the play's characteristics—its "realism," its questioning of heroism—are contrary to the epic genre as understood in Shakespeare's time, so that there is a problematic tension in the play between the "epic" and the "antiepic." This tension is, I think, real and significant, and the controversy it has occasioned is responsibly directed. Accepting the customary terms of the question, I would say that it is possible to understand and admire the epic-antiepic tension as a solution to the special moral problems presented by the play's subject and the audience's attitude to it.[12]

In dealing with the question of genre it is not necessary to accept the customary terms, however; one may in fact put the question in terms much more germane to the investigation being carried out here. Thus we might say that a major operative tension exists between the Chorus's kind of speech action and that of all the other characters. Direction of address seems the most relevant feature. The Chorus's action is directed out toward the play's audience, like that of an epic narrator. His position is thus, of course, different from that of the chorus of classical Greek drama. There is no question of his addressing other characters in the play; he stands quite outside the fiction they comprise. It is this distinctive feature of the Chorus's speech action—his direction of address—whose significance I shall, in a somewhat roundabout fashion, try to assess.

[11]See, for example, Richard David, "Shakespeare's History Plays."

[12]The genre tension seems to reflect the disparity between the audience's and Shakespeare's attitude toward nationalistic militarism. The battle of Agincourt for the audience would have been an example of glorious heroism worthy of epic, and their view would have been too strong to be denied directly in the play. But Shakespeare, with his customary skepticism and lack of sympathy for military exploits, goes a long way toward countering and modifying that view. The only actual engagement in the "glorious" battle he presents is, after all, Pistol's capture of a Frenchman. My understanding of this aspect of the play was aided by a lecture of Professor Joseph Kramer.

Much has been written about the change in dramatic assumptions involved in the movement from the Elizabethan to the proscenium stage. Part of the change has to do with the audience's separation from the action and the rise of the "fourth wall" illusion which did not obtain in Elizabethan drama, where various sorts of interchange between actors and audience were possible and even usual. The aside to the audience is one example. Natural enough on Shakespeare's stage, it comes to seem paradoxical and therefore less viable on the proscenium stage. Interestingly, it seems less viable there than that other famous and similar Elizabethan convention, the soliloquy—disappearing earlier and not returning, as in the Symbolist drama, with the soliloquy.[13]

The difference in viability has important implications for the dramatic experience. It nicely separates the fourth wall from the naturalistic or realistic illusion: aside to the audience violates primarily the former, while soliloquy not addressed to the audience violates only the latter. The difference, then, suggests that conventions involved in the fourth wall illusion—those of direction of address in particular—play a more immediate part in the audience's experience, and therefore in the dramatist's art, than do conventions of realism or verisimilitude.

As far as the texts are concerned (there may have been extemporaneous speech), the clearest example of the Elizabethan dramatic characters' turning address from each other to the audience is probably the aside. But some soliloquy may also have been addressed to the audience. In fact, without the fourth wall convention, the only speech action that could *not* be addressed to the audience is that which is addressed otherwise—to another character or, in apostrophe, to someone or something else. Thus, as was noted in Chapter 1, much of Richard's soliloquylike speech could be played as directed to the audience.

The fourth wall convention eliminates such address to the

[13]I say that the aside "seems" rather than "is" less viable than the soliloquy because there seems to be no comprehensive comparative study of the prevalence of the two devices in each period of the drama with which to verify my impression. (The claim made in Chapter 1 that length is the only essential difference between aside and soliloquy does not really contradict the argument here; for there I use the terms slightly differently—not, as here, to distinguish direction of address.)

audience and may indeed be defined by this function. Thus this sort of address becomes problematical during the period in which Shakespeare is produced exclusively on the proscenium stage, the very physical shape of which suggests and gives a name to the convention by which address to audience is outlawed. In other words, the fourth wall leaves the characters of a drama more to their own devices; specifically it means that their speech is more exclusively directed to each other.

These not unfamiliar views are set forth here in order to get at a rather elusive quality of *H5*. For the Chorus in this play seems to function as a proscenium, his speech enclosing the main action and separating it from the audience so that something like the fourth wall convention obtains in the speech action.

The Chorus produces this effect in a way quite different from the proscenium stage, of course. The latter eliminates address to the audience by way of an imaginary physical barrier. In *H5* the possibility of address to the audience is, as it were, precipitated out of the main action and localized in the speeches of the Chorus. But the resultant effect is the same: in the main action the possibility of address to the audience is ruled out to a degree unusual for Elizabethan drama.

This in turn means that the main body of the play becomes in a sense more exclusively dramatic than the earlier plays of the tetralogy. To the extent that the Chorus siphons off the possibility of address to the audience, the remaining characters are thrown on each other, and their speech action is more necessarily interaction than that in the earlier plays of the tetralogy.

In this respect the Chorus has a function and significance like that of the messages of *H5* discussed above. Both further and emphasize the completion, in the main drama, of a development we have been tracing through the tetralogy, away from the undirected speech of Richard II to a realm of directed, practical, consequential, "dramatic" (a term we shall return to in Chapter 6) speech action presided over by Hal.

IV

Most of the preceding description of the general quality of speech action in *H5* pertains naturally to Hal himself, the single character whose speech dominates the play. He is, however, much more than an example of these general qualities, and therefore I want now to concentrate on what, within the realm of the play, is significantly distinctive about his uses and conceptions of language.

The elaborate and impressive description given in the opening of the play by Canterbury—

> Here him but reason in divinity,
> And, all-admiring, with an inward wish
> You would desire the king were made a prelate:
> Hear him debate of commonwealth affairs,
> You would say it hath been all in all his study:
> ·
> . . . that, when he speaks,
> The air, a charter'd libertine, is still,
> And the mute wonder lurketh in men's ears,
> To steal his sweet and honey'd sentences;
> So that the art and practic part of life
> Must be the mistress to this theoric
>
> (I.i.38–52)

—is an introductory summary, directing attention to what is to be unfolded in the rest of the play. It might, on the surface, seem odd that the archbishop should lavish such praise on the mere verbal prowess of the new king and that this verbal prowess should be the sole specific evidence provided as proof of Hal's reformation. But in the context of the preceding plays such a direction of attention seems almost inevitable.

Canterbury provides a kind of official recognition and praise not only of Hal's verbal prowess but also, as we have said, of the variety and flexibility of that prowess. In terms of the Babel metaphor he claims that in Hal himself the proliferation of tongues has become cause for rejoicing. Canterbury uses the Fall metaphor explicitly to introduce this praise:

> Consideration like an angel came,
> And whipp'd th' offending Adam out of him,
> Leaving his body as a Paradise,
> T' envelop and contain celestial spirits.
>
> (I.i.28–31)

Having seen in *2H4* the direr consequences of the loss of
Richard's linguistic Eden, we are now to see in Hal's language a
transcending of those consequences.[14]

As in the two preceding plays Hal himself frequently remarks
upon the subject of language and speech action (though,
perhaps because of the high events underway, his remarks may
be less noticeable); and, as before, it is possible to deduce something of a "theoric" for him.

He shows an assured and sophisticated appreciation of what
Austin calls "illocutionary force" in naming a large variety of
speech acts; furthermore, via messenger in

>Unless the Dauphin be in presence here,
>To whom expressly I bring greeting
>>(II.iv.111–12)

and directly in

>we give express charge that in our marches through the
>country there be nothing compelled
>>(III.vi.112–13)

he touches on the subject of explicitness in speech acts. (Thus
"we give express charge" is a kind of super-performative, making explicit the making explicit of the illocutionary force.) All this
applies a conception of speech as action and interaction and also
a consciousness of third-person audiences. In this respect we
see in Hal here a synthesis of the antithetical views of Richard
and Henry IV—Richard's limited cognizance of the audience of
his speech, Henry IV's limited cognizance of his interlocutor.

Alternatively, when Hal speaks of speech as creation of verbal
constructs, it is in scorn:

>these fellows . . . that can rhyme themselves into
>ladies' favours. . . . What! a speaker is but a prater; a
>rhyme is but a ballad.
>>(V.ii.159–63)

In this respect he stands in direct opposition to Richard, who

----

[14]The third "summary metaphor" of the end of the Middle Ages may also be
implicit, in Canterbury's "came reformation like a flood" (l. 33).

typically thought of language as a material for the construction of verbal objects such as rhymes.[15]

Hal's linguistic "theoric" is in fact the opposite of Richard's in several ways. Whereas Richard's conception of language made it difficult, painful, and destructive for him to perceive the limits of his command, Hal has a firm grasp of the matter. When he says

> We may as bootless spend our vain command
> Upon th' enraged soldiers in their spoil
> As send precepts to the leviathan
> To come ashore
>
> (III.iii.24–27)

and

> O be sick, great greatness,
> ·
> Canst thou, when thou command'st the beggar's knee,
> Command the health of it? No, thou proud dream
> (IV.i.257–63)

he shows his understanding that speech acts take place in the world and are thus subject to limitation and failure; that verbal action like nonverbal action is finite.[16] His scorn for rhyme is matched by, and shown in the same speech as, his scorn for "these fellows of infinite tongue" (V.ii.160); and this too reminds us of Richard's conception of language.

Throughout the tetralogy the topic of name has been a convenient index of changes in the prevailing conception of language. In *H5* remarks such as Hal's rather offhand

> as I am a soldier,
> A name that in my thoughts becomes me best
> (III.iii.5–6)

---

[15]Indeed, Hal's "prater" may echo the description by York in *R2* (V.ii.23–28) of Richard as an actor whose "prattle" is tedious. The word is not common in Shakespeare.

[16]More specifically, it is the fact that speech acts occur in a social world of conventions, a world of what Searle calls "institutional facts," that makes them subject to failures of the sort Austin calls "infelicities." Both the hypothetical speech acts dismissed by Hal involve Austin's type A.2 infelicity (v. *How to Do Things with Words*, p. 35ff.).

seem to be at the tetralogy's greatest remove from Richard's virtual obsession with name. The distance we have come is also shown by the fact that naming is not a kind of speech act very frequently mentioned by Hal.

The kinds he does mention most frequently are *telling* and *saying*, which have to do with the messages discussed above. And after these, the kinds he mentions most notably and frequently are *vowing, swearing, taking an oath*, and other variants of the promising we have seen him concerned with in the *H4* plays.

This much "theoric" and more is manifested in "the art and practic part," that is, in Henry's own speech action, to which we now turn, considering it from the standpoints of (1) illocutionary force and (2) direction of address.

1. *Illocutionary Force*

Henry's consciousness of speech as action and his awareness of the variety of kinds of speech acts are reflected generally in the kinds of speech act he performs. As far as illocutionary force in concerned, his speech in *H5* has a variety, flexibility, and virtuosity that is unique in the tetralogy. Within this variety there are discernible unifying trends or tendencies.

Not only does Henry frequently speak of the acts of vowing, swearing, and the like, but also, even more frequently, he *performs* these acts, so that their predominance is significantly characteristic of his speech action. All these acts are like promising, which had been characteristic of him earlier in the tetralogy, and which continues to be so in *H5*; indeed they are in a sense official and solemn kinds of promising, and such forms of the basic characteristic act befit the new role of kingship.[17]

But in *H5* no single act such as promising—even with variants such as vowing, swearing, and the like—looms so large in Henry's speech as promising did before. In this play the quantity and variety of his speech is such that one needs to relate promising to other characteristic acts to determine the sim-

[17]While it is true that vowing or swearing, unlike promising, *could* be a matter of representing that *p* (i.e., that something is the case), with Hal they are typically commitments to do some act A.

ilarities and assess their significance. Thus to generalize from promising we need to bring it into the clearest possible focus. Here John Searle's analysis is helpful.[18]

In this "full dress analysis of the illocutionary act" (l. 54), Searle takes promising as his "initial quarry, because as illocutionary acts go, it is fairly formal and well articulated" (l. 54). His method is to formulate rules which in sum amount to necessary and sufficient conditions for an utterance, X, to be a promise.[19] He arrives at four basic types of rule:

> *Propositional content:* future act A of speaker S
> *Preparatory:* (a) hearer H would prefer S's doing A, and
> S believes that this is the case
> (b) it is not obvious to S and H that S will
> do A in the normal course of events
> *Sincerity:* S intends to do A
> *Essential:* the utterance of X counts as the undertaking
> of an obligation to do A
>
> (ll. 57–67)

Searle then argues (with examples) that *any* illocutionary act can be analyzed in terms of these four types of rules.

Searle's analysis is built upon Austin's, and is aimed at correcting Austin's admittedly provisional typology of illocutionary force. Whereas Austin had hoped for a classification of "general *families* of related and overlapping speech acts" (*How to Do Things with Words*, p. 149), Searle is less sanguine:

> we must not suppose, what the metaphor of "force" suggests, that the different illocutionary verbs mark off points on a single continuum. Rather, there are several continua of 'illocutionary force.'
>
> (*Speech Acts*, p. 70)

But Searle's analysis does not amount to complete atomism, for it remains possible to define classes or families of illocutionary acts which are identical or similar with respect to one or several of the principles of distinction, though they may be dissimilar

[18]In *Speech Acts.*
[19]More precisely, rules for the use of an illocutionary-force-indicating device, such as "I promise," or "This is a promise."

with respect to others.[20] For instance, the very closely related family that is characteristic of Hal—vowing, promising, swearing, giving one's word, and the like—would seem to have identical rules for propositional content, sincerity, and essential condition, and to differ only (and only slightly) with respect to the preparatory rules.

Delineating an extended family of which this immediate family is part—finding, that is, a category which includes a larger portion of the illocutionary acts performed by Hal—necessarily involves decreasing the similarity between members of the family. Here the most useful procedure I have found is to concentrate on the propositional content. Maintaining Searle's rule for promises (vows, etc.), that is, *future act of speaker S*, and allowing the other rules to vary freely, we can include Hal's many serious and playful threats in the extended family. Restricting the propositional content rule to *future act*, we can enlarge the family to include those acts whose propositional content is a future act of the hearer—for example, Hal's orders, commands, requests, urging, exhortation, advising, entreaties, and so on—and also acts whose propositional content is a future act of a third person—for example, his striking predictions, prophecies, and warnings.

This class, illocutionary acts whose propositional content is a future act, includes a remarkably large portion of Hal's verbal action in the play. And its predominance seems to distinguish Hal not only from other characters in the play but also from the two preceding monarchs in the tetralogy. The concentration on acts, in particular, distinguishes Hal from Richard, whose domain was a timeless one of essences and necessities. Concentrating on action, Hal shows himself a practical Renaissance Lancaster and that his domain is the finite fallen one of time and will. The concentration of futurity, on the other hand, distinguishes Hal from Henry IV; and it is in a sense how Hal redeems the time of the Lancastrian world. The fall of Richard's untensed world gives way to the world of time, but it is as if a complete tense system is then "discovered" piecemeal, rather than at a

---

[20]Since *Speech Acts* Searle has developed a further classification of illocutionary acts in "A Taxonomy of Illocutionary Acts," one of a number of recent competing taxonomies.

stroke, in *H4* and *H5*. In the "justling time" of *1H4* the "justling" present tense is discovered—comes into use in thought and speech. The next tense to be discovered is of course the past, in the retrospect of *2H4*. The urgency of the present and the burden of the past are as much as Henry IV can absorb; and it is a great deal. But the limitation is clear and serious. The world of time is also a world of futurity. A tense system without a future tense is incomplete and therefore in a sense without meaning. It is in *H5* that the tense system is completed, and so becomes comprehensible. Hal, through his concentration on futurity, redeems time by making tense significant. Balancing retrospect with prospect, he completes the conceptual system in which present action has meaning.

2. *Direction of Address*

The direction of Hal's address is typically made explicit by vocatives and pronouns. Thus the status of his verbal action as interaction is emphasized, and he is notably distinguished from Richard, who tended toward soliloquylike speech not explicitly directed to his auditors. Having shown us the fall of Richard's world of undirected or universally directed speech, having shown us in the two parts of *H4* the ensuing release of vigor and festivity increasingly eclipsed by a sense of disorder, uncertainty, and diminution, until deafness threatens to vitiate interaction almost as much as Richard's verbal absolutism had done, Shakespeare now gives us a king who redeems the time and speech which is directed with an assurance, explicitness, and flexibility new to the tetralogy.

These qualities are especially impressive when Hal changes direction of address in a single speech, as at II.ii.79ff., when he berates and sentences Scroop, Cambridge, and Grey. The speech begins with Hal's addressing the traitors:

> The mercy that was quick in us but late
> By your own counsel is suppress'd and kill'd:
> You must not dare, for shame, to talk of mercy;
> For your own reasons turn into your bosoms,
> As dogs upon their masters, worrying you.
> (II.ii.79–83)

In five lines we have five second person pronouns, making very emphatic the direction of address, as though to give the traitors no hope of slipping away. Having thus as it were impaled them, Henry exhibits them to the court:

> As dogs upon their masters, worrying you.
> See you, my princes and my noble peers,
> These English monsters!
>
> (ll. 83–85)

The abruptness of this change of direction of address — the utter lack of any polite or respectful signal of his turning away from the traitors — manifests Henry's authority and also his disgust and contempt. Suddenly reducing them from second to third person, Henry excludes them from interaction with him, making them mere objects of discourse.

The effect is accentuated when Henry next names

> My Lord of Cambridge here
>
> (l. 85)

transforming the usual polite vocative form with the deictic "here" into a disdainful third person. The movement of objectifying the traitors and separating himself from interaction with them continues as Henry speaks of Grey

> This knight, no less for bounty bound to us
> Than Cambridge is, hath likewise sworn
>
> (ll. 92–93)

without even deigning to use his name. The brevity is part of the withdrawal as though Henry now disdains even to speak about the traitors, much less to them. But this proves the climax of the movement of withdrawal, for Henry now changes direction of address again, turning from his court to Scroop:

> But O,
> What shall I say to thee, Lord Scroop? thou cruel,
> Ingrateful, savage and inhuman creature!
>
> (ll. 93–95)

This introduces the long address to Scroop which ends

> I will weep for thee;
> For this revolt of thine, methinks, is like
> Another fall of man.
>
> (ll. 140–42)

The speech ends with a final change of direction of address when, in

> Their faults are open:
> Arrest them to the answer of the law;
> And God acquit them of their practices!
> (ll. 142–44)

Henry turns conclusively and authoritatively away from the traitors.

Henry's irony, a feature of speech action which has been characteristic of him through the *H4* plays and which distinguishes him from Richard and Henry IV, is also a manifestation of his control of direction of address. In his first words about the gift of tennis balls, for instance,

> We are glad the Dauphin is so pleasant with us;
> His present and your pains we thank you for
> (I.ii.259–60)

the thanking is ironic. That is, Henry performs the act without meaning it. It is a real thanking but an insincere one, and Henry intends the insincerity to be recognized—perhaps by the ambassador and certainly by the nobles of his own court.

Such ironic verbal action is only an extreme form of Henry's typical consciousness of audience—of the impression he makes on auditors other than the person he is addressing. At the same time, however, he is also typically well aware of his interlocutor. His speech, that is, never seems to be *merely* for the sake of overhearers. And when there is no audience of overhearers, as in his courtship of Katherine, it is no less effective.

Finally, there are two special directions of address worth noting in Henry's speech. Both are new for him, and both further distinguish him from the earlier monarchs in the tetralogy.

The first is that of the "we happy few" speech (IV.iii.18–67)[21] and other addresses to the English army. In such speech, directed toward a group and emphasizing the unity of the addressees, the "we" is almost as strongly inclusive as can be

---

[21]Or at least the direction of address to the end of this speech as it is usually understood and played. The speech begins directed to Westmoreland, and could conceivably be entirely so addressed.

imagined; hence it is as far removed as possible from Richard's "we" which, it will be remembered, was so exclusive as not even to be a plural.

The other special direction of address is that of prayer directed toward God, in Henry's

> O God of battles! steel my soldiers' hearts;
> Possess them not with fear
>
> (IV.i.295ff.)

before the battle of Agincourt. This serves, I think, to emphasize the distance between Henry's world and the Absolute: it *removes* God from the world of the play's action. Richard had been more Adamic, had talked confidently about God as though He were close and understandable. But when Henry addresses God in prayer or ascribes the victory at Agincourt to Him (thus, in a sense, finally permitting the kind of contest that Richard began the tetralogy by refusing), he shows his appreciation of the limitation of human action, an awareness which is part of his own effectiveness.

V

In *H5* the variety of languages which had been excluded from Richard's absolutist conception of language and had then increasingly been a symptom of the limitations of Bolingbroke's reticent practicality becomes a prominent example of the manageable order of the world. Language barriers are no less real than spatial ones, and overcoming them is as pragmatic a matter as sending a message. Whether across barriers or not, verbal action in *H5* is directed to an addressee. It is communicative and hence not merely action but also consequential interaction. Thus, after the perversions and deformations of the speech-situation in the three preceding plays, in *H5* the speech-situation is almost entirely what we think of as normative or normal. This results partly from the framing of the action by the Chorus; but even more from the predominance of Hal's characteristic use and conception of language—all along he has learned and used a variety of tongues as media in which he performs directed verbal acts.

The predominance of Hal's conception and use of language

means in a sense that strictly linguistic problems are no longer very serious. With the mystery having gone out of them, the problems that remain prove manageable, so that language itself approaches being a neutral and transparent medium for action. But such a reduction in the importance of language means that speech action performed in that medium becomes more important. That it is performed in language, and in a particular language, must be taken into account, and is; but now the mysteries and problems of verbal action are those which attend any action. I conclude with a single example of this effect.

In the last act, as Hal achieves his perfection as man and king, the Babel theme of language differences is, as we have said, emphatically present—in the treaty and, more extensively, in the wooing. In the treaty the bilingual vocative with which the French king is to address Hal in messages stands as a kind of emblem of Hal's linguistic realm, of his solutions to the old problems. In the wooing we see those solutions put into practice, and there language becomes prosaic; in the medium itself there are no mysteries.

There are mysteries, however, in the verbal action. When Hal says of the speech act which in the course of the tetralogy has been most characteristic of him

> 'tis hereafter to know, but now to promise
> (V.ii.222–23)

he shows, as he has done repeatedly, his awareness of the limitation of verbal action. Yet here (and, I think, almost exclusively here) he is not only showing his awareness of that limitation but also poignantly exemplifying it. It is a moment of "dramatic" irony sharper, more sudden and extreme, I think, than any other in Shakespeare:

> *King Henry.* If ever thou beest mine, Kate, as I have a
>   saving faith within me tells me thou shalt, I get thee
>   with scambling, and thou must therefore needs
>   prove a good soldier-breeder. Shall not thou and I,
>   between Saint Denis and Saint George, compound a
>   boy, half French, half English, that shall go to
>   Constantinople and take the Turk by the beard? shall
>   we not? what sayest thou, my fair flower de luce?
> *Katherine.* I do not know dat.

> *King Henry.* No; tis hereafter to know, but now to
> promise: do but now promise, Kate, you will
> endeavour for your French part of such a boy, and
> for my English moiety take the word of a king and a
> bachelor.
>
> (V.ii.211–26)

The mystery and wonder is, of course, in the distance between
this playful, sanguine promise and the future to which it refers:

> Henry the Sixth, in infant bands crown'd King
> Of France and England, did this king succeed;
> Whose state so many had the managing,
> That they lost France and made his England bleed.
>
> (Epilogue.9–12)

And such mystery depends less on the fact that Henry's action
—his "promise"—is verbal than on the fact that acts verbal
and nonverbal are performed, finite and temporal. It is the
mystery shown in the paradox of the Chorus's final mention
of Hal:

> Small time, but in that small most greatly liv'd
> This star of England.
>
> (Epilogue.5–6)

CHAPTER FIVE

Method

Since the method of the preceding four chapters is partly unconventional, it seems in order to attempt a theoretical description of that method, to describe its relation to those of some other criticism of the tetralogy and, more generally, to some methods of prominent recent Shakespeare criticism. "Method" itself is slippery enough to justify a little anchoring and stabilizing by defining it in terms of the object of attention or of the evidence adduced. The study of imagery constitutes one method, the study of meter another—an idealization, of course, but a fairly standard and serviceable one.

Part of the method of the preceding chapters is quite conventional, at least for the twentieth century. This is the consideration of what is said *about* language. Taking as its object of attention references within the plays to a single subject or idea—that of language—it is a "thematic" approach. That the particular pieces of evidence used and the arguments based thereon differ from those of other studies may justify this one; nevertheless, this part of the study is of a relatively familiar kind.

Applied to the Lancastrian plays, this method has usually concentrated on the theme or subject of politics, or on a special topic like majesty, though there are notable exceptions such as L. C. Knights' study of *2H4*, "Time's Subjects," in *Some Shake-*

spearean Themes. Thematic criticism of other Shakespeare plays has, of course, concerned itself with a very wide variety of topics.

In two respects, though, the otherwise conventional thematic approach I have used is perhaps slightly unconventional. First, the consideration of the theme of language is linked to, articulated in terms of, the fact of dramatic character.[1] This has not been an absolutely rigid program, but more than is usually done I have structured the discussion of the theme of language in terms of the personages of the plays.

Also somewhat unconventional is that the preceding thematic study of language is not predominately or even to a large extent concerned with imagery. Thanks in part to the example of G. Wilson Knight, for whom "themes" virtually amount to patterns of imagery, there has been a close link between the two in recent Shakespeare criticism. However, though imagery may be the main embodiment of certain themes or topics, and I have tried to take into account and discuss where appropriate the language-imagery of the plays, it is not the main embodiment of the theme of language in the Lancastrian tetralogy (nor, probably, anywhere else in Shakespeare): the overwhelming majority of references to language are not what we would call "imagery."

A word should also be said about the thematic rubrics used above—the analogues of Fall, Babel and Renaissance. My arguments have not depended on taking them as anything more than convenient summaries of certain aspects of the overall design of the tetralogy, though my use of them may have suggested otherwise—that these analogues operated in Shakespeare's mind in ways similar to here. To decide whether this is the case is beyond the scope of this study; but I can at least try to clarify the matter a little before leaving it.

There is a distinction to be made on the status of these analogues between the Babel story and the Fall and Renaissance "stories." The latter two seem clearly "in" the tetralogy. (Grounds for this assumption are in the one case the correspon-

[1]Such an articulation of the theme is more than a convenience—see pp. 162–63 in this chapter, and Chapter 6.

dences worked out by Tillyard and in the other a different set of correspondences supported by explicit allusions, within the text, to the Fall.) But, since each of these two stories is itself (like the tetralogy) about much more than language, the fact that they are inherent analogues of the overall action does not yet show that they are inherent analogues of the part of the design with which we have been concerned, the subject of language. To show this would obviously involve extensive argument of a complex sort.

The case is somewhat different with the Babel analogue. Here we have a story much more centrally concerned with the relevant subject of speech and language. And, since here the "fit" is extremely good (as we have seen), and since Shakespeare must have known the Babel story well, one is inclined to suspect that the analogue was at least in the back of his mind as he wrote the tetralogy. Such suspicions could be verified by explicit allusions to the Babel story, but as it happens there are none in the tetralogy nor, apparently, anywhere else in Shakespeare. In default of explicit allusions, one may look for implicit "submerged" ones and find them. I have noted some passages which might qualify in this sense.[2] Such evidence, however, is no more than suggestive.

Thus what we have done with each of these summary metaphors, beyond using them to order a complex body of data and argument, is to raise but not answer the question of their inhering in the tetralogy.

We are mainly concerned here with the unconventional part of the preceding study, the part having to do with dramaturgy, the part that takes speech action as the object of attention. This part of the method is unconventional inasmuch as "speech action," as I have used the concept, is itself somewhat unconventional, being (as explained in the Introduction) a modified version of the theory set forth by J. L Austin in the 1950s, first

[2]Such possible submerged allusions to the Babel story include the long play with the Parable of the Builder in *2H4*, Falstaff's dying talk of the Whore of Babylon (one of two mentions of Babylon in Shakespeare), his dying "babbling," the mentions of Assyrians in *2H4* and *H5* (the only ones in Shakespeare), the several appearances of the word "tower," and so on.

widely published in the mid-1960s and only more recently used in literary criticism.[3] I hope the preceding chapters have demonstrated some of the practical utility of the notion; now I want to consider it more abstractly and to place its use in relation to certain recent approaches to Shakespeare.

The importance of Austin's idea of "speech act" for literary criticism (as also, I believe, for linguistic philosophy) is a function of what it stands opposed to. The matter may be put thus: for Austin, "action" is a general category including both verbal acts—speech acts—*and* nonverbal acts. His view (call it "view A") stands in opposition to the view ("view B") that "action" is not such a general category, but rather that it is by definition nonverbal. According to view B, "speech" and "action" are correlative coequal opposite categories; while in Austin's view A we find that "speech" is a subcategory of "action," and its opposite correlative is "nonverbal action." Though these views are opposed, there seems to be little point in arguing that if one is correct the other must be incorrect, for such an argument would involve hopeless simplification. But it is worthwhile to consider where and how these views are manifested.

Perhaps the most notable manifestation of Austin's view is at the lowest most fundamental conceptual level possible: in the bedrock of the language itself, in which words like "promise" and "command" are coequal with words like "kill" and "walk" in being verbs and in being equally replaceable by the generic "do." Thus the structure of the language itself might lead us to suppose that Austin's view is the natural, standard, customary one.

Yet it is the opposed view, B, which seems to prevail at higher conceptual levels—even when we consider the level represented by proverbs, which, by virtue of the folk production and transmission and the brief single units involved, we might expect to have the same conceptual pattern as the language

[3]Explicitly speech-act criticism first appears in the early 1970's. Among earlier Shakespeare criticism which at least touches on my concerns here, see C. L. Barber's treatment of naming and the magic use of language in the Lancastrian tetralogy in *Shakespeare's Festive Comedy* and Maynard Mack's treatment of *Hamlet* and *Lear* as plays dominated by the interrogative and imperative moods respectively in "The World of Hamlet" and *King Lear in Our Time,* p. 89ff.

itself.[4] The situation seems the same at much higher levels of conceptualization, in particular at that level represented by Shakespearean criticism, where the overwhelming trend is to use "deed," "action," and the like only to mean nonverbal action. To be sure there are unsystematic exceptions, but in general when a Shakespeare critic speaks of *action* he means *nonverbal* action. It is against the effects of this conceptualization's prevalence that Austin's usefulness should be measured.

In the prevailing view B the isolation of nonverbal action under the neat and positive rubric "action" has been useful in the study of stage production. And the concurrent exclusion of reference to action from the idea of language seems to have facilitated appreciation of what can generally be termed "poetic features" of the language of the plays—for example, patterns of iterative imagery, which appertain to the plays as language constructs, language-things made by Shakespeare.

Nevertheless, I think that this prevailing view has attendant disadvantages which can be seen to affect Shakespeare criticism from the seventeenth century down to the present. They have to do with the separation of the ideas of action and language. In particular, it seems that the view B has made it needlessly difficult to consider speech as action, with something of a dilemma as a result. On the one hand there are scholars and critics who deal with methods and significances of stage production. While they have much to say about nonverbal action on stage—stage

[4]As in the following representative list from Morris Palmer Tilley's *A Dictionary of the Proverbs in England In the Sixteenth and Seventeenth Centuries*:

(D186) Deeds are fruit, words are but leaves
(D187) Deeds are male (men), words are female (women)
(D394) Do as I say, not as I do
(D402) It is better to do well than to say well
(S116) It is sooner (easier, better) said than done
(S117) No sooner said than done (So said so done)
(S119) Saying and doing are two things
(S121) Saying is one thing and doing another
(S122) Say well and do well end with one letter, say well is good but do well is better
(S123) Say well is good but do well is better
(W797) Few words and many deeds
(W800) Fine words dress ill deeds
(W812) Good words without deeds are rushes and reeds
(W820) Not words but deeds

business, entrances and exits, demeanor, and so forth—they
seem to pay comparatively little attention to the language itself.
They employ theoretical machinery designed to deal with nonverbal action, which in a sense, is inadequate for examining the
language of the work.

Harley Granville-Barker is one of the most distinguished and
ablest practitioners of this mode of criticism. Concerning himself
with stage production, he yet devotes much attention to the
language of the plays, more than do most other stage-oriented
critics. And what he says about language is, within its limits,
extraordinarily perceptive. Yet these limits are very narrow.

They are set out in the introduction to the first series of
Prefaces to Shakespeare:

> The dialogue of a play runs—and often
> intricately—upon lines of reason, but it is charged
> besides with an emotion which speech releases, yet
> only releases fully when the speaker is—as an actor
> is—identified with the character. There is further the
> incidential action, implicit in the dialogue. . . .[5]

These—the emotion with which the dialogue is "charged" and
the implicit "incidental action"—are virtually the sole categories
of Granville-Barker's critical attention to the language of the
plays. By "incidental action" he means nonverbal action—
essentially the bodily movements (gestures, postures, position
with respect to other actors, etc.) of the actors. He is, of course,
very adept at deducing this implied action (and since the *Prefaces*
a great deal more such deduction has been undertaken, aided
especially by the conclusions of scholarly research into Renaissance stage production). Since even in Shakespeare, however,
stage business is very far from continually implicit in dialogue,
this must remain a subsidiary concern, except where it shades
into the major category of Granville-Barker's critical attention to
the dialogue, of which for him "the emotion which the speech
releases" is a virtually continual feature.

His terminology is apt: it is the speeches which express—
"release"—the emotion, and not the characters. He is typically
concerned with unintentional, involuntary, or unconscious re-
velation of emotion. The paradigm seems to be that X qualities

---

[5]Granville-Barker, *Prefaces to Shakespeare*, 1:5–6.

of Y's speech Z reveal that he has the emotion W. Verbal features are thus symptoms of the emotion or state of mind, and so represent a kind of continuous cueing for nonverbal action.[6]

This concern with emotion is quite in line with Granville-Barker's famous view that "the text of a play is a score waiting performance."[7] For emotion is the easiest part of the mind of the fictive character for the actor to represent, in manner and demeanor, in performance. In a sense, though, this concentration entangles Granville-Barker in self-contradiction.

The "charged" emotion "released" in performance amounts, after all, only to the *manner* in which the action is performed. Now, with speech acts as with nonverbal acts there is a relation between the manner and kind of act in a given situation; but there can hardly be any simple general rule that allows us to deduce the one from the other. In analyzing a specific passage Granville-Barker always, I think, takes as obvious or self-evident the nature of the illocutionary act (e.g., whether a character is warning another or merely reminding), whereas what is in question for him is the emotion with which the act is done (e.g., warning desperately or ccntemptuously). Yet, as preceding chapters should have suggested, given a specific text the illocutionary force of the speech act may be quite as open to question as the emotion. If Shakespeare does not provide stage directions like "*Macbeth (gloomily)*," neither does he provide directions like "*Macbeth (making a resolution)*." And *both* sorts of direction are of concern to a performer of the part. Thus Granville-Barker's concentration on manner as revealed emotion involves him in making unjustified assumptions about the text as a score for performance.

This limitation of the approach seems most apparent in discussions of the characters and their interplay. When, for instance, we are told that Lear's

> When she was dear to us we did hold her so
> But now her price is fall'n . . .

is a "bitter gibe to Burgundy,"[8] we have confidence in the "bitter" because we have seen elsewhere in Granville-Barker how

[6]Granville-Barker also at times uses linguistic features to deduce something like quality of mind, or character.

[7]Granville-Barker, *Prefaces*, 1:5.

[8]*Ibid.*, p. 285.

sensitive and how convincingly argued such assessments are. The "gibe," however, does not elicit such confidence.

In the sections of the *Prefaces* on "The Verse and Its Speaking," where Granville-Barker concentrates most on the language of specific passages and of the entire play, the limitation of his approach is clearer and more severe. Typically here it is the mere phonetic features of the language—the pattern and texture of vowels and consonants, accents, pauses, and so on—that he considers. This too is in line with his notion of the text as a score waiting performance, since phonetic texture is the dimension of language most obviously reminiscent of music. But even within this dimension the musical-emotive qualities of local sound constitute a narrow focus; and phonetics itself is only the lowest level at which language can be analyzed.

Thus the theater-oriented criticism of Granville-Barker represents, in its inadequacies and limitations, one horn of the critical dilemma which seems to result from the prevalence of view B, the conception of speech and action as opposite terms. For Granville-Barker, interested in acting and "action" (i.e., "action B"), is driven, unnecessarily and in contradiction of his own stated aims, to disregard all linguistic features except those most obviously and directly appertaining to the characters' implicit nonverbal activity.

The other horn of the dilemma is much more widely represented—by those critics who (also holding view B) concern themselves with the speech, or speeches, or language,[9] of the plays—because the *materia* for investigation is much richer and more extensive than the *materia* of features pertaining to non-

---

[9]*Speech-speeches-language* represents an ideal and in large part a historical evolution of this direction of attention. Discussing a character's *speech*, for instance, what Falstaff says on such-and-such an occasion, or on many occasions, is to come very close to "view A," that is, to considering the speech as action. This, however, seems an unstable position which tends to modulate into the consideration of *speeches*, for instance, "This royal throne of kings, this scept'red isle. . ." But this too seems unstable: an uneasy and usually unsatisfactory middle ground between view A (a speech is after all delivered by a certain character in certain circumstances) and view B (but it is nevertheless a linguistic object constructed by Shakespeare which can be so appreciated). A fairly stable position is reached when a critic attends to the *language* of a play; in so doing he concentrates on those linguistic features which have least to do with action, and he may largely ignore questions of character and situation.

verbal "action." This century has seen the creation and use of a rich and varied conceptual machinery for dealing with the language of the plays. For our purposes the work of G. Wilson Knight seems most usefully to exemplify this critical direction, because it is widely known and appreciated and, its idiosyncracies nonwithstanding, constitutes a fairly pure and comprehensive type of language-oriented Shakespeare criticism.

In the essay "On the Principles of Shakespeare Interpretation,"[10] Knight sets forth the program of his approach both in this book and, with increasing refinement, subsequently. At this point his program is clearer and more thoroughgoing with respect to what does not interest him than to what does. A few of his refusals (e.g., to concern himself with sources) do not matter to us. Most of them, however, do, for, though Knight justifies them variously, most—his refusals to attend to character, to "the temporal dimension," to the "story," and to the fact that the works are dramas—are manifestations of a thorough exclusion of the notion of actions from the conceptual framework used to interpret the plays.

What does concern him is put here as "the spatial dimension," "the atmosphere," the place of each play in "the Shakespearean progress," and "also the minor symbolic imagery of Shakespeare, which is extremely consistent."[11] What Knight here calls "minor" represents in fact the increasing preoccupation of his books on Shakespeare, and the area of study for which he is probably most noted.[12]

Knight and others have commented on limitations in his approach, but these are more severe than is recognized: they seem to distort the text more than is admitted, and finally to be arbitrary inasmuch as they are by no means necessitated by Knight's stated aim—"to reveal that burning core of mental or spiritual reality from which each play derives its nature and meaning."[13]

[10]*The Wheel of Fire.*
[11]"On the Principles," p. 16.
[12]It also represents a direction of attention which for four decades has been used increasingly by critics and students, has become so familiar as almost to be standard, and perhaps now has begun to wane in prevalence—following an evolution roughly coinciding with, and involved with, that of the "new criticism."
[13]"On the Principles," p. 15.

This statement comes as a surprising justification for ignoring the genre, in a paragraph which begins with Knight's separating himself from such theater-oriented approaches as Granville-Barker's:

> Nor will a sound knowledge of the stage and the especial theatrical technique of Shakespeare's work render up its imaginative secret. True, the plays were written as plays and meant to be acted. But that tells us nothing relevant to our purpose. . . . Shakespeare wrote in terms of drama, as he wrote in English. In the grammar of dramatic structure he expresses his vision; without that, or some other, structure he could not have expressed himself. But the dramatic nature of a play's origin cannot be adduced to disprove a quality implicit in the work itself. . . . Therefore it is not necessary . . . to remember, or comment on, the dramatic structure.[14]

The argument here seems to turn on an implicit equation of "theatrical" with "dramatic." And this equation seems to discredit the notion of "dramatic structure" by reducing it to something only incidentally and contingently associated with the text. So discredited, the dramatic structure may even be spoken of as a "grammar" without our being expected to take the metaphor very seriously. The chain of irrelevance by association can then be extended to language itself. If dramatic "grammar" seems to need apologetic quotation marks, so does the grammar of English—it too becomes as incidental, extrinsic, as far removed from the text before us as the Globe Theatre.

However much he might like to, Knight in beginning to interpret a text cannot, of course, ignore the grammar of the language any more than could Shakespeare in writing the text.[15] The most abstracted patterns he discovers are profoundly verbal and therefore grammatical. But he can and does more easily ignore "dramatic structure" because this seems to him finally to concern only theatrical production with actors moving about on a stage, that is, to concern only (nonverbal) "action."

[14]*Ibid.*, pp. 14–15.
[15]The length of Knight's textual citations—they seem to average five or six lines—does allow him to ignore many grammatical considerations.

Austin's theory can help clarify our assessment of the limitations of Knight's approach. In a sense any nondramatic work constitutes a single monolithic speech act, having, in the first place, one speaker (the narrator, expositor, "poet," or whatever) and one direction of address. Furthermore with nondramatic works we can often name a single illocutionary force for the entire work—such as the force of narration. None of this holds for drama. There is no way to describe an entire drama as a single speech act; there is no single speaker who is the doer of the action. But this is to say that speech action, and features of speech action, are *at issue* in drama, at issue because variable and indeterminate. Indeed one might suggest a version of Aristotle's formula based on Austin: "speech action is the soul of verbal drama."

The inadequacy, then, in methods such as Knight's may be put thus: the features of language attended to in such a method, not being features of speech action, are not features essentially and distinctively at issue in the genre of drama. When speech action is dealt with in such a method (and it is of course dealt with to some extent), it is done so unsystematically and by the way.

Thus in Knight and Granville-Barker we have two sides of a critical dilemma that results from the prevalence of the view B that speech and action are correlative opposites. This view has aided both critics, as any categorization may do, by concentrating and directing investigation. But it has also hindered them. In a sense, Granville-Barker's method would be adequate and comprehensive if the texts were elaborate directions for mimes, Knight's if they were elaborate meditative lyrics. And the two approaches naturally tend to distort the works in such directions. But Austin's view A, and the rich conceptual framework he and his followers provide for dealing with speech acts systematically, provides a way of resolving the dilemma.[16]

[16]It might be objected that too much time has passed since the major work of Granville-Barker and Knight for their positions to be useful in triangulating ours, and that the inadequacies we find in their approaches are by now fully recognized and understood. This may partly be the case. However, while the generation of Knight and Granville-Barker defines itself in opposition to Bradley, attending carefully to (real or supposed) inadequacies in his method, the next generation does not so typically define itself by opposition to such critics as Knight and Granville-Barker—whose (real or supposed) inadequacies have thus

Analysis of the plays' language as speech action seems furthermore to bear significantly on the idea of character in drama. The question of how to deal with character has been important in Shakespeare criticism generally (especially recently, with the late-nineteenth-century "psychological" excesses and the early-twentieth-century reaction) and in the criticism of the Lancastrian plays in particular (with Morgann's 1777 essay on Falstaff practically initiating the intensive critical analysis of character, as well as initiating a line of disputation about all the major characters of the tetralogy which has lasted down to the present). Arthur Sewell, in *Character and Society in Shakespeare* (1951), has surveyed the theoretical groundwork of the idea of dramatic character, clarified the matter, and enunciated firm and positive conclusions which are especially valuable as regards the uncertainty about character that has marked the criticism since Stoll.

Particularly helpful is Sewell's emphasis on the indissolubility of character and action in drama. His description of this distinctive feature of the genre is nicely complemented by the analysis put forth recently by Scholes and Kellogg.[17] According to them, the essential characteristics of a narrative are that it has a story *and* a teller of the story, whereas drama has a story *without* a teller. In narrative, which includes all the nondramatic kinds of presentation of a story, character is revealed in action, but it may also be revealed—stated, vouched for—by the teller. And since in narrative the teller's evaluation has authority over our own evaluation of character as revealed in action, character is separable from action.[18]

---

not received such careful attention as Bradley's. Therefore it seems right, if one *is* concerned to place oneself in opposition to others, to choose the generation of the thirties, and thus to place oneself not only with respect to them but also to the long dialogue in which they were, in a sense, the last answerers.

[17]In *The Nature of Narrative.*

[18]Even with a "fallible" or limited narrator we still must go through him—we take his bias into account, allow for it, and *then* trust his authority. One main reason for the separability of characters from action in narrative is the fact that narrative can give us thoughts, emotions, and the like, of characters directly. Whether or not there are such things as thoughts in real life, they exist in narrative fiction, and can be presented simply by the narrator's saying "John thought 'X.'" This makes narrative enormously different from drama in which, as in real life, we must deduce mental states *from* action.

In drama, however, where there is no authoritative teller of the story, character is revealed *only* in action. (Even if character B describes character A, it remains true that B is himself part of the action; thus his description is part of the story and does not have the authority of the teller in narrative.) This absence of authority in a sense makes drama more difficult for its audience, and in Shakespeare criticism there is the occasional tendency to avoid the difficulty by devices which in effect deny the genre and treat the plays like narratives. Stoll himself seems to do this at times. Sewell's virtue is that he refuses this short cut, insisting that we take the genre for what it is and meet its exigencies head-on.

The difficulty of this task is partly a result, I believe, of the fact that most of the action in a play of Shakespeare's is verbal, for whose description we have had little theoretical machinery. But with the machinery now provided by Austin and his followers, it seems possible to get at what is distinctive and thus characteristic in the verbal action of dramatic characters. This does not necessarily entail a naturalistic conception of character; the descriptions I have attempted of the various personages of the tetralogy are not especially naturalistic or psychological. What it does entail is taking all the language of drama as characteristic action, at least in the first instance—a more radical proposal than it may sound. It means, for instance, delimiting the subject of style in dramatic language more sharply than is customary. For, in the first place, there is in a sense no such thing as a Shakespearean or Marlovian style, but only Falstaffian, Hotspurian, Tamburlainian styles. And, in the second place, questions of style—questions, that is, of the general manner in which verbal acts are done—are less important than those bearing more directly on the acts themselves, such as the kind of act, its direction, force, and so on.[19]

The preceding discussion of my approach and its application in the previous four chapters involves, of course, a particular notion of what drama is, one which can be put in terms of the

[19]"Style" is relative, of course: there are deep and surface styles. We think of style as the *manner* in which something is done; but if a certain thing is done often enough, in a sense it becomes part of the style or manner. See also Richard Ohmann, "Instrumental Style."

defining, essential features of the genre. The first part of my working definition is conventional: drama is a literary entity. That is to say, I am concerned with a verbal entity embodied in performance, in other words, with "drama" rather than "theater." Herein my approach differs from that of Granville-Barker and other theater-oriented critics and is like that of Knight. But whereas Knight takes the plays simply as literary entities, and so develops an approach at least equally applicable to other genres, I am concerned with drama as a literary genre, with what distinguishes it from other literary entities. And in this my working definition is partly unconventional.

We can consider this working definition as a modification of the Scholes and Kellogg notion of drama as a story without a teller (we are justified in our modification since they suggest it not as a categorical definition but by way of clarifying the nature of narrative). "Story" begins to distinguish drama from other genres such as lyric; and one assumes the presence of a story in dealing with drama—at least with most pre-twentieth-century drama, and certainly with Shakespeare. As plot, "story" is that feature usually attended to in definitions and theoretical discussions of drama from Aristotle to the present, and also usually by Shakespeare critics whose approaches, like mine, involve working definitions of drama as a distinctive literary genre. Bradley is an example. Yet "story" does not distinguish drama from narrative, and much of the ostensibly "dramatic" theorizing about features of story like climax could and does apply equally well to narrative. Altering "story" to "sequence of action" brings us closer to what we seek; let us, however, leave this part of the definition aside for a moment.

"Without a teller" is awkward for our purposes because it is a negative formulation. Here, however, is the approach to a positive one. Knowledge of the language is the first *sine qua non* of making sense of a drama, and reflects the fact that a drama is a literary entity. The second *sine qua non* is a knowledge of the speech headings, the fact that in drama the entire text (excluding the speech headings and further stage directions) is assigned to a group of characters by whom it is understood to be spoken. This would seem to be the first and the essential division or articulation of the whole, logically well preceding and far more basic than such diversions as act and scene, climax and dénouement, major plot and subplot. It is, in fact, a characteristic of drama so utterly basic, and therefore so obvious, that it seems to have been largely ignored in theoretical discussions of the genre. Yet because it is so basic it can provide a satisfactory working definition of "drama."

With slight further alteration, "without a teller" can be seen as a negative version of this positive formulation. The trouble with "without a teller" is that by the word "tell" it too suggests narrative. Removing this narrative coloring gives us something like "drama lacks a (single) speaker or sayer of it." This is equivalent to what I take to be an essential feature of drama as a literary genre, the fact of the text's assignment to a group of speakers, and begins to be a satisfactory definition for distinguishing drama from other literary genres.[20]

One might object that "assignment to a group of sayers" could apply to choric odes or first-person-plural narrative voices. These, however, can be excluded easily by saying that the speakers of a drama speak separately and in succession. Yet even thus refined the definition would still cover literary works which are not dramas, such as the Bible, *The Sound and the Fury*, Pound's *Cantos*. What we need here, then, is something like Scholes and Kellogg's "story" or our "sequence of action." With this we can complete our working categorical definition, as follows.

A drama is a sequence of acts, verbal and nonverbal, done by a group of characters to or on each other. The text of a drama consists of stage directions which may indicate either verbal or nonverbal action, or the locale, or almost anything else germane to the action. The remainder of the text consists of the "speeches" and the speech headings which assign the speeches to the characters. The "speeches," the bulk of the text, consist of the words *in which* the verbal action is done. The "locutionary acts"—the acts of saying such-and-such a thing—are thus perfectly and completely represented by the text. "Illocutionary acts" *may* be completely and perfectly represented; this occurs

[20]*Assignment to a speaker or to a group of speakers* would seem also to begin to be a feature for distinguishing what we think of as "literature" from other linguistic constructs, because it rules out, for example, the telephone directory.

when they are made explicit—as by a performative, or conceivably by a stage direction. Otherwise they are *implied* by the text; and the same is true of nonverbal action which is not indicated by stage directions.

It may seem that in explicating this working definition of drama we have strayed rather far from Shakespeare's Lancastrian tetralogy, into the hinterlands of general dramatic theory. As will now be apparent, though, our discussion is not so ambitiously disinterested after all. Rather, the "working definition" of drama I have presented abstractly here is, in fact, suggested by the course of the tetralogy itself.

CHAPTER SIX

❀ Conclusion

I

Using the method just discussed we have, in Chapters 1 to 4, considered ways in which the Lancastrian plays are about language and verbal action. Though dealing with the four plays separately, we have been able to see some of the deep unity of the whole tetralogy—how the subject of language and speech action constitutes part of the tetralogy's unity as a large aesthetic whole. It is this matter, necessarily subordinate until this point, to which we now turn. We shall be viewing what we have already seen from another standpoint. Specifically, I will argue here that the tetralogy is about language with respect to the genre of drama, that the verbal form, drama, is itself a major unifying subject or theme of the tetralogy.

This way of understanding the work needs a little preliminary explanation—not, I think, because it is especially difficult, but because it is somewhat unfamiliar.[1] To see the tetralogy as being about drama does not mean taking the work as an allegorized poetics any more than to see it as being about kingship means taking it as an allegorized political tract; nor is it to suppose that dramatic art is what the tetralogy is "really," at base, essentially, about. Nor on the other hand does it necessitate timidly restricting oneself to commentary on passages in which the subject of

---

[1]Though this way of viewing the text may be found occasionally in much Shakespeare commentary, the only systematic application of it seems to be James L. Calderwood's *Shakespearean Metadrama*.

drama is handled explicitly—theatrical performances within the plays, appearances of the theater metaphor, or words like "actor," "play," and the like—any more than considering the theme of kingship would necessitate limiting attention to the analogous passages.

The "metadramatic" theme (the term comes from R. J. Calderwood[2]) does, however, pose certain problems because of its reflexiveness. To say that the tetralogy has a metadramatic dimension is in a sense to say that it is its own subject, and this seems potentially bewildering.

Among the things such a claim might mean, two are especially likely. One (A) is that a given play is about the comparatively general exigencies, rules, and categories of which any play, including the one under consideration, is only a single instance—that the play is about the dramatic art of which it is an example. The other (B) is that the play is about the unique confrontation with the exigencies of the genre undergone by the author in creating that play—that the play is about itself as an instance of dramatic art.

The distinction has less to do with what is observed (since much the same evidence would support either claim), or even with what is made of it, than with *how*. The attendant risks differ. It is (B), with its perfect reflexiveness, that seems more likely to lead to bewildering paradox and bedazzlement. The merely proximate and incomplete reflexiveness of (A) is protection against such dangers; the risks here would rather be those that attend any statement of thematic significance—such familiar and prosaic dangers as *missing the point*.

R. J. Calderwood very gracefully makes both kinds of claim about *R2*, [3] and means both, sometimes indistinguishably, by "metadramatic." Here, though both seem valid for the tetralogy, we shall try to keep (A) to the fore—for the sake of clarity, and because it seems wise to eschew the special headiness of (B) in a discussion as abstract and summary as ours must be.

The special claim made here is further limited and defined by the evidence used, the preceding discussions of the four plays. Thus I want to show, not that the tetralogy in every respect is

[2]Op. cit.
[3]In "The Fall of Speech," his chapter on *R2*.

about the genre of drama, but merely that the tetralogy, in being about language and speech action in the ways described above, is (also) about drama.

II

The question of the subject's importance—the question of whether it is really "in" the tetralogy—remains. The work is obviously about kingship; just as obviously, it might be argued, the work is *not* in any important sense about drama, since the subject is mentioned only in a handful of passages. Calderwood provides one answer to such objections:

> What I am most anxious to demonstrate . . . is simply a way of looking at Shakespearean drama that perhaps brings into relief a territory of meaning which Shakespeare could hardly have ignored and which we as critics might well explore.[4]

Another kind of answer must be my discussion itself—and the extent to which it is applicable. There is also a third kind of answer.

The period of the Lancastrian tetralogy is the only time in Shakespeare's career for which we can be fairly sure that he was thinking of drama as a literary genre distinct from others, first, because the tetralogy spans approximately the period in which he was writing nondramatic works as well as plays.[5] In writing brief lyrics and long narratives side by side with plays he would presumably have been thinking about the less obvious differences between these genres. One may assume this merely by virtue of the depth and penetration of his mind with respect to literary matters. Furthermore, one would assume that the differences between literary genres, and specifically the features of

[4]*Shakespearean Metadrama*, p. 20.
[5]The exact chronology of the canon is of course not yet certain, but minor variations among suggested chronologies do not affect the argument here. For the tetralogy, I accept the dating by E. K. Chambers in *William Shakespeare: A Study of Facts and Problems*, which gives 1595–99 for *R2–H5*. The narrative poems were published in 1593 and 1594 and seem to have been written shortly before that; the sonnets seem to have been written in the early and middle 1590's, though they were not published until 1609.

drama that distinguish it from others, were of especial moment to him as he wrote the Lancastrian plays, for it was just then that he was deciding to devote himself to drama exclusively. It is not only important that he worked in other genres during the Lancastrian period, but also that thereafter he did not.

Such a preoccupation with the nature of drama, implied by the variety of genres undertaken in the period, would, one assumes, be manifested *within* the works themselves. I suspect that one could discover numerous such manifestations—various, interesting, and subtle ones. Here I mention only a particularly striking example, the "play-within-plays" which, like the nondramatic work, date from approximately the same period as the Lancastrian tetralogy.[6] "Plays" is of course not an entirely accurate term for this miscellaneous group of theatrical productions ranging from the "ostentation, or show, or pageant, or antic, or firework" of "The Nine Worthies" through Hal's and Falstaff's "play extempore," and culminating in "The Murder of Gonzago."

Still, the borderline cases seem just that; the group defines a territory that centers about the genre of drama, as that later group of theatrical productions, the masks and staged dreams of the romances, does not.

It thus seems right to suppose that Shakespeare in writing the Lancastrian tetralogy was preoccupied with those attributes of drama which distinguish it from other literary genres; and it seems likely that this preoccupation would be manifest in the tetralogy—and not merely in the play within the play of *1H4*. Now, among the differences between literary genres which Shakespeare presumably considered are those features of language peculiar to the various genres—those raised into prominence by the choice of one genre over another. In particular, it seems likely that the context in which he saw—took and meant—the tetralogy's theme of language and speech action is that of the idea of the genre of drama.

The foregoing is offered not, of course, as *proof* that the subject of language in the tetralogy, which we have seen to be of

---

[6]Plays within plays appear (with Chambers's chronology) between 1594 and 1601; and in comparatively full form in *Love's Labour's Lost, A Midsummer Night's Dream, 1 Henry IV,* and *Hamlet.*

major importance in and of itself, has a metadramatic significance, but rather by way of support based on circumstantial
evidence for the claim now to be elaborated. We shall be moving
once more from *R2* to *H5*; but since here our focus is the tetralogy as a whole we can move freely back and forth among the
plays when it seems appropriate

III

The metadramatic argument of *R2* described by Calderwood deals with apparently inherent disparities between (1) the
qualities of language valued in nondramatic poetry and (2) the
exigencies of the genre of drama. Specifically, Calderwood finds
that in *R2* Shakespeare is coming to terms with an apparent
degradation that poetic language must undergo in drama. "The
Fall of Speech" in *R2*, he finds, is Shakespeare's relinquishing of
the speech of nondramatic poetry.
  I am in accord with this much of his treatment of the play
within the context he has chosen, that of the four earlier plays
Titus Andronicus, Love's Labour's Lost, Romeo and Juliet, and *A
Midsummer Night's Dream.* In certain respects, though, his treatment does not do justice to the metadramatic argument of *R2* as
part of the tetralogy. His neglect of the linguistic world that rises
as Richard's falls (discussed in detail above, Chapter 1), for instance, blurs the design of the tetralogy.[7] I proceed, then, from
that part of his argument with which I am in accord, the idea
that Richard's fall manifests Shakespeare's relinquishing of a
nondramatic linguistic world.
  Although, as we have seen, the notion of Richard as a poet
figure is unsatisfactory, it is true that his conception and use of
language are like that of a (decidedly) nondramatic poet, so that
his linguistic world is that of nondramatic literary genres.
Richard thinks of language as a substance for the construction of
verbal objects rather than as a medium for verbal acts; he regards his own speech not as verbal action but rather as the

---

[7]Calderwood's acceptance of the speech-vs.-action dichotomy, as when he
speaks of "the contrary tendencies of the verbal (or retarding) and the actional
(or progressive) elements of dramatic art" (*Shakespearean Metadrama,* p. 15) also
blurs the metadramatic design of the tetralogy.

utterance of verbal objects. The direction of address of his speech tends to be "univocal," unmarked, as with the authorial voice in nondramatic genres. And in his linguistic absolutism he considers his voice to have the sort of authoritativeness which accompanies the voice of the nondramatic author.

In these ways, what Richard embodies—what he *is*, in a sense—is the same conception and use of language we find in the *Sonnets, Venus and Adonis,* and *The Rape of Lucrece.* "Appropriately" embodied in those poems, this linguistic world functions, stands to outlast marble or gilded monuments. But embodied in Richard, in a drama, it falls. Richard falls, as it were, because he is simply not equipped to survive in his genre, not equipped even to comprehend it.

IV

If, undeterred by the oddity of regarding Richard as the linguistic world of nondramatic literature embodied disastrously in a dramatic character, we pursue the notion further, it turns out surprisingly to account for some of his most familiar and characteristic ways of talking about language.

Supposing that Richard would have *R2* be a nondramatic literary object, how might his wish be granted with the least effort and least alteration of the text? Narrative is the obvious genre into which we would convert the drama. The stage directions are already narrative in form, of course, and we might then suppose that by adding a somewhat expanded group of stage directions to the "lines" we would have the entire play converted very easily for Richard's sake into his "sad tale."

What we *would* have is what *R2* is when it is performed. The story, however, would not yet even be comprehensible: not until we assigned the speech by converting the speech headings of the drama into narrative additions like "Richard said . . . then Bolingbroke said. . . ."

The point here is that *name,* as speech heading, is categorical in drama, as it is not in other genres. We, of course, value Shakespeare for the (mainly verbal) action of the play, for the "text" which is the subject of critical comment; no one would think of admiring the speech headings. But without the column of names alongside the "text" the play could not be performed or comprehended. Metadramatically the character "Richard" consists of a few stage directions and a selection of the poetry of *R2* determined by the placing of the speech headings. Thus his name, with which he is virtually obsessed in the fictional world of *R2*, is, in the form of speech heading, a categorical limit of his voice entailed by the genre in which he exists, a limit which cannot be accounted for from the standpoint of his own non-dramatic language. Richard, as it were, does not know what name to call himself because he cannot read *R2* with its speech headings. At moments, though, as when he asks

> What must the king do now? . . .
> . . . Must he lose
> The name of king?
>
> (*R2*, III.iii.143–46)

he seems obscurely aware that there is a dimension of his existence in which *"King."* changes to *"Rich."* as *"Bulling."* becomes *"King."* [8]

V

It might be objected that when Richard says

> Thus play I in one person many people
> And none contented
>
> (*R2*, V.v.31–32)

and in other explicitly metadramatic passages he seems to be linked so strongly to the genre as to contradict what we have just said. In these passages, at least, far from being a figure of nondramatic literature, he might seem almost an avatar of drama. This inconsistency, I want now to show, is only apparent, though it does derive from a part of Richard's metadramatic significance which we have not yet touched on.

In the first place, the suggestion of dramatic prowess in "Thus play I . . . many people" looks like an example of Richard's characteristic overestimation of his own power, especially when we set it against York's

[8]Speech headings from the facsimile (*Shakespere-Quarto* facsimiles, no. 18, London, 1888) of the copy of *R2* Q1 now in the British Museum.

> As in a theatre the eyes of men,
> After a well-grac'd actor leaves the stage
> Are idly bent on him that enters next,
> Thinking his prattle to be tedious;
> Even so, or with much more contempt, men's eyes
> Did scowl on Richard
>
> (*R2*, V.ii.23–28)

in which the transfer of the nation's (and, metadramatically, Shakespeare's) allegiance is put almost emblematically in terms of a stage metaphor. This, by suggesting that it is a kind of inferior drama that falls with Richard's fall, moves us in the right direction; but the matter can be clarified further.

When Richard speaks of playing many persons and when York likens the change of allegiance to an audience's reaction to different players, we are dealing with plays to be sure, but more as theatrical than as dramatic entities. These metaphors, and indeed most of the stage metaphors in Shakespeare, are probably better termed "metatheatric" than "metadramatic." The fact that Richard is like a player, thus, does not mean that he is dramatic; it means that he is theatrical.

Since both "theatrical" and "dramatic" normally apply to plays there has not usually been cause for maintaining the distinction very clearly; and to do so would have been even more difficult for Shakespeare than for us because his English did not yet have a familiar word with which to categorize what we mean by "drama."[9] Nevertheless, we ought here to clarify the distinction because, far from being merely academic or terminological, it is one of Shakespeare's central concerns in the Lancastrian plays.

We can do this by imagining defective or aberrant plays to which one or the other adjective would apply exclusively, most simply, perhaps, by imagining stages which would preclude either adjective. On the one hand, a play performed on a kind of cellblock set consisting of several rooms open to the audience but having no access to one another, with one actor in each room, might be very theatrical (showy, histrionic, etc.), but it would not be dramatic because there could be no interaction

---

[9]According to the *OED*, "Drama" appears in 1515, "dramatic" in 1589, and other forms of the word still later.

among the characters. On the other hand, if we remove the walls separating the players from each other and erect a real wall in place of the imaginary "fourth wall" between the players and the audience, we have a set on which a play might be very dramatic (full of conflict, etc.), but it would not be theatrical because its audience could only see a wall.

Richard's language is theatrical and nondramatic because those same features that make his linguistic world like that of nondramatic literature also preclude his engagement with other characters in the drama, thus putting him in the position of an actor on our imaginary cellblock stage. And, thus deprived of dramatic grounds for his existence, his theatricality hypertrophies.

This stage of affairs is evident, for instance, in his problem of identity. Identity in a play has both a theatrical and a dramatic dimension; but the dramatic seems more important: a character exists, is defined dramatically through interactions with others. Lacking this kind of definition, Richard's identity becomes problematical and, as if to prove or establish his existence, he theatrically parades his emotions. Indeed all the features we have noted (such as his characteristic explicitness) with which Richard in his speech action takes into account and tries to create an audience, at the expense of engagement with his addressee, are linguistic correlates of his being a nondramatic theatrical player.

This position, which is thus not at all contradictory, is characteristic of Richard throughout the play and is finally realized physically, much as we have done with our imaginary stage, when he soliloquizes in his cell.

VI

The metadramatic significances we thus find in the character Richard are all implicit in York's "As in a theatre . . ." (quoted above, p. 174). The envisaged theater and the appeal to sight (i.e., the emphasis on appearance) define the bounds of Richard's world, the basis of his existence. His nondramatic language, powerful and beautiful in its own terms, might seem ideal for a theater because of its theatricality, but because he exists in a drama, it becomes "tedious prattle"—the genre renders it so. Richard's language cannot be judged on its own terms because there are other terms, other speakers—in particular, the "well-grac'd actor" Bolingbroke.

An interesting thing about York's theater metaphor is that it does not begin sooner, since there is so much ground for it in his preceding description of the nation's acceptance of Bolingbroke:

> You would have thought the very windows spake,
> So many greedy looks of young and old
> Through casements darted their desiring eyes
> Upon his visage.
>
> (V.ii.12–15)

The theatrical metaphor is, of course, built on this ground when York proceeds to speak of these eyes "idly bent" on Richard, but considering how natural it would have been a moment before, the Homeric sonorousness of the metaphor's introduction seems awkward.

The awkwardness is hardly enough to trouble us; it does, however, seem to manifest the different metadramatic significances of the two kings. The theater metaphor here *must* in a sense be restricted to the theatrical Richard, and can only apply by default to Bolingbroke—to a Bolingbroke who has left the stage—for, as we shall see, his realm is not theater but drama. Furthermore the metadramatic focus properly, if a bit awkwardly, begins to apply where it does because a tediously prattling Richard is there contrasted with a well-graced actor who, for all the metaphor tells us, may have said nothing. The metaphor can thus encompass Bolingbroke the "silent king." These two explanations for its slight peculiarity are not unrelated, for Bolingbroke is dramatic by being silent. His silence is more dramatic than Richard's speech, in a quite specific way.

In genres other than drama silence can be talked about. A narrator may tell us that someone was silent, a poet may describe silence. Or an expositor may be "silent" about a specific matter—but then he will be talking of something else. These things are possible in drama, too, but there silence can also be presented quite as directly as speech: it exists, is present, whenever a character onstage is not speaking. For silence is structural in drama, an actual part of the work's ordering determined by the speech headings. This becomes apparent if we realize that that ordering could also (though less economically) be accomplished by "silence headings," lists of the characters onstage to whom each portion of the text is *not* assigned.

We have seen various ways in which Richard's linguistic world seems more suited to other literary genres than to drama. It is nevertheless true that the distinctive qualities of his speech can also exist in drama—Richard is, after all, a character in a play. But with Bolingbroke's silence we have a quality that is *exclusively* dramatic, possible in drama and not in any other literary genre. Richard is silent at times, to be sure—as it were, under the duress of the genre. But Bolingbroke's silence is emphasized and characteristic. Thus his assumption of the throne brings into prominence an aspect of speech action which is uniquely and essentially dramatic.

This much of the difference between the two kings points out the direction of what seems to be the tetralogy's basic metadramatic argument, which we may now state loosely as follows: the tetralogy figures, enacts, manifests the rise of the genre of drama out of, and in opposition to, nondramatic literature. Or, to put it slightly differently, the tetralogy is about a shift of allegiance from nondramatic to dramatic literature.

VII

In the *H4* plays the "metadramatic" theme continues, the tetralogy continues in various ways to be about theater, about plays as they are produced before audiences. For example, Richard's problem of the relation of appearance to identity—involving the fact that in theater appearance is, in a sense, everything—continues to be treated in various guises in these plays. Generally, though, and particularly with respect to the subject of language, questions of theatricality become less important after Richard's fall, when allegiance is owed to a king whose language is as untheatrical—reticent, inexplicit—as it is dramatic.

It is not merely Henry's silence that makes him more dramatic than Richard. His conceptions and uses of language are themselves dramatic in that the features they take into account and raise into prominence tend to be those particularly at issue in drama. Whereas in Richard's speech the nature of the act—the illocutionary force—was usually theatrically explicit, in Henry's speech the direction of the act—the direction of address—is usually dramatically marked. When his mind is on language it is typically on language as used in speech and, furthermore, speech which is converse, the verbal interaction that constitutes drama. The control he exercises within verbal interchanges is dramatic; and large movements of the plot consist of his using his royal prerogative to halt and disbar one kind of interchange with Hotspur and to bring into being another kind with Hal.

These aspects of what we might call Henry's verbal practicality not only are dramatic in themselves, but also force, so to speak, all the language of his plays to be dramatic. His silence and reticence allow the same thing to happen: other voices can and must come alive and into play. When Henry leaves the stage and our eyes are "idly bent on him who enters next," we find not "tedious prattle" but the drama of "justling" voices.

The "justling" makes a design fundamentally different from that of *R2*. "Our plot," says Hotspur,

> is a good plot, as ever was laid . . . a good plot,
> friends, and full of expectation: an excellent plot, very
> good friends . . . .Why, my Lord of York commends
> the plot, and the general course of the action.
> (*1H4*, II.iii.16–22)

Within the fiction he means the rebels' plans but, since his praise also applies to the overall design of *1H4*, it bears comparison with the "lamentable tale of me" envisioned by Richard (*R2*, V.i.44). Whereas Richard's "tale" is explicitly nondramatic—explicitly narrative—Hotspur's "plot" is potentially and, in this case, actually, dramatic. And where a "tale" may be about a single person (as is the case with Richard's "tale of me"), "plot" entails that multiplicity of persons to whom the language of drama is assigned. The two ways of considering "story" are realms apart. Hotspur's comes from a realm whose dramaticality overflows, as it were, into playacting within the play. And this playacting is itself dramatic, as Richard's theatrical playing was not, because here what matters is the liveliness of the interchanges, with one speaker pitting himself against another.

VIII

1H4, with Falstaff, Hotspur, Henry, and Hal, with Boar's Head hijinks and Shrewsbury heroism, seems inspirited with the excitement and vigor released by Shakespeare's having decisively abandoned the responsibility entailed by univocal literary genres and given, at least for the moment, wholehearted allegiance to drama. The sense of release comes from the greater ease of the genre: in it each character speaks for himself, in his own way and in his own terms, so that the author is absolved from the obligation of discovering a single voice in which to make a complete, perfected utterance. In *1H4* the fact that all the language of a drama is assigned to one of a group of speakers, none of whom has the comprehensive authority of the teller of a tale, is accepted and used to create a cast of characters unprecedented in Shakespeare for variety, vividness, and depth. In *2H4*, however, this fact about the genre is regarded with a cooler eye. The justling voices begin to seem like the confusion of Rumour's tongues.

With all the languages of the work assigned by speech headings—that is, with all the language being characteristic speech—there seems to be no verbal standard for judgment, so that unity and significance seem not to be locatable. The justling of the atomistic array of speakers can be controlled in varying degrees by Henry or Shakespeare. But control does not solve the problem of criteria for judgment and assessment when, among a variety of voices, each speaks with nothing between itself and the audience and thus seems to claim for itself the kind of authority that accompanies the comprehensive voice of nondramatic genres.

A dramatist might gloss over these difficulties by, for instance, toning down and blurring distinctions among the voices to make the question of judging between them less apparent. Shakespeare does the reverse. The tongues proliferate, grow vividly, profoundly distinct and idiosyncratic.[10] Thus the Babel theme, coming increasingly to the fore throughout the tetralogy, manifests the special problems of the notion of character in drama.

Character in drama, we could say, is a function of plot and thus under the control of the playwright. This is true but deceptive because it may consider "plot" as Hotspur does—as a kind of scorecard of machinations, deaths, battles, and the like, as a plot *summary*. However, in ways I have tried to show above (Chapter 5) drama is in a sense all and only plot. Dramatic character, then, is a function of every speech and nonverbal act, irreducibly, so that the problem of judging between the array of speakers (and thus the problem of discovering the significant unity of the work) cannot turn on the outcome of a battle. Henry's kind of control of Hotspur's kind of plot falls short of giving a significant unity to the various voices' contradictory appeals.

Therefore, even though the extreme tension in *1H4* between (1) this sort of control and (2) dramatic character is itself an attractive interim solution to the problem of dramatic unity, we must move beyond it. In *2H4*, with Hotspur dead and Henry dying, as the voices proliferate and make their claims relatively unimpeded, Shakespeare admits and presents a radical, intrinsic, and distinctive problem of the genre: the threat to the unity of the work occasioned by the various voices' being received by the work's audience directly, unmediated.

Falstaff, of course, is the crucial case here. In *1H4* it is his voice that grows most lively in spite of the Henry-Hotspur kind of plot control—even, as it were, mocking such order, pretending to be Henry and to have killed Hotspur. And in *2H4* it is with Falstaff that Shakespeare raises most forcibly the possibility that unified significance is simply not achievable in the genre. With his "whole school of tongues in this belly of mine" (*2H4*, IV.iii.18) echoing the tongues of Rumour, Falstaff is virtually emblematic of his world of drama seen in extremity as a Babel.

The problem is not that Falstaff through the *H4* plays appeals

[10]Exaggerated superficial language differences among speakers appear in most of the plays of the genre-conscious Lancastrian period; and it seems possible that in most cases the device has metadramatic significance.

to the other characters (as he does, in both senses of the word), but rather that he appeals irreducibly to us. His appeal is even addressed to us in a sense, for, as we have seen above (Chapter 2, pp. 73, 110), his speech is characterized by an implicit address of sorts to the play's audience. And his appeal is problematical because it seems to vitiate the drama from within.

I say "from within" because Falstaff is dramatic as Richard was not. He does not, like Richard, suppose that his word has the power of the authorial voice in nondramatic genres—he claims, indeed, that words are "air." And, again unlike Richard, Falstaff can engage other characters. Whereas Richard flourishes and is most himself in extended monologue, Falstaff flourishes when he has an interlocutor; he seems to need one, even such a token one as the Boy. Yet with Falstaff as with Richard, problems of judgment arise because of extradramatic address and a theatrical appeal. And when, with walls of "deafness," Falstaff separates himself from other personages of the drama, his play becomes like that performed on the theatrical and nondramatic cellblock stage postulated above. Thus an essential feature of the genre of drama—the fact that its characteristic tongues make their appeals to us directly, without mediation—seems increasingly, as we follow Falstaff through the *H4* plays, to mean only confusion and disunity.

IX

In *2H4* a progressive laying open of difficulties produced by the very nature of the chosen genre is also implicit in Shakespeare's handling of the subject of time. We have seen in preceding chapters that Richard's "I wasted time and now doth time waste me" is a fairly comprehensive summary of his characteristic conception and use of language; and we have seen time become an increasingly important and problematic term in the linguistic world of Henry IV's reign. The change of allegiance from Richard to Bolingbroke is analogous to the Fall, as we have seen, in being a change from a timeless to a temporal world; the historical metaphor puts the same change in another guise: from Richard's medieval faith in eternal verities to the Lancastrian world in which the idea of historical time is "discovered." [11] This movement also has metadramatic significance. The general admission in *2H4* that all the characters are "time's subjects" embodies, I suggest, a recognition that drama itself, as opposed to other genres, is "time's subject."

Richard's "I wasted time" may apply to incongruities between his language and his literary genre. Limited by his non-dramatic language, he has wasted not only his lifespan within the fiction but also the "two hours' traffic" his stage will bear. He discovers that he is in a play in the nick of time—only minutes before the play is over and the audience goes home.

What Richard discovers, though, seems too simple to account for the brooding on time in *2H4*. The implication seems to be merely that he should have exercised more active control sooner. And this is precisely what his successor does in *1H4*. With the problem thus solved, how can we explain *2H4*?

The answer, I think, is that here as in other respects Richard is able to appreciate the nature of the genre only to a limited extent. It fits in with what we have already seen of him that the time-bound aspect of plays which he recognizes is more a theatrical than a dramatic fact, since it derives from the limits of a theater audience's attention. And this limit is in fact temporal only if the drama is staged. As far as the text is concerned—that is, regarding drama as a literary form—this amounts only to a roughly determined length, a feature which does not set drama apart from all nondramatic genres. [12]

The point is that drama is more radically, essentially, and distinctively time-bound than Richard is quite able to comprehend, because its story has no teller. In narrative, however much the "story" is temporal, there is a kind of Edenic timeless

[11]The overall metadramatic argument of the tetralogy considered here could, incidentally, be given its own historical guise and taken as a special case of Tillyard's historical metaphor: the *historical* rise and predominance of the genre of drama in the English renaissance. It does seem likely that the historical meaning of the work should pertain to literature as well as to the political and social developments with which Tillyard was concerned. However, as should be clear, the metadramatic argument as described here is idealized and abstract, and not at all historical.

[12]It is interesting that closet dramas seem conventionally to observe the same length restrictions.

place occupied by the narrative voice;[13] but if we take a story from narrative into drama this point of Edenic stability is lost. A narrator, as we know, may begin *in medias res* and, from his timeless vantage point, move wherever he pleases in the story, so that the order of presentation of the parts need have nothing to do with time. But in drama the order of presentation of the story's parts is strictly temporal. The events of Act II *must* be later in the time of the story than those of Act I.

The frequent recounting of events from the past in *2H4*, then, seems to embody a longing for the eternal vantage and the freedom from the order of temporal sequence afforded by narrative. Yet the various narrators' nondramatic use of language does not establish a frame of atemporal stability for drama any more than Richard's attempts did. The result is simply that the "story" of *2H4* is a story of people's telling stories—because narration in drama is merely an act in a succession of other acts.

This leads us to the observation that drama is bound to time not only in the large—the "plot"—but also in the small: the language of drama is radically temporal. At those points in the text at which the special qualities of dramatic language become most apparent—for example, where the speaker changes direction of address, or where one speech ends and another begins—it is just there that, were we converting the work to narrative, it would be necessary to make additions in the narrative voice to specify temporal order: "Hal said . . . *then* Falstaff said. . . ." We would specify the temporal order because in narrative it is not predetermined; we *could* have said "Falstaff said . . . and, before that, Hal said. . . ."

Such moments force on our attention the fact that *all* the language of drama is radically temporal, that within a single speech the language is bound to temporal sequence since at any point the speech *could* stop, be interrupted, or change direction of address. If it continues without such changes, it is because the speaker persists: "Hal says . . . and then Hal says. . . ."[14] The

[13]The narrator's position seems Edenically timeless because his order of presentation is independent of the temporal order of his story, as discussed below, and also because the time of his act of narration is typically unspecified.

[14]Recent "affective criticism" seems to want to give a roughly analogous temporality to all literature, dramatic and nondramatic, via the notion of the experience of reading the text.

absence in drama of a vantage position from which one may cordon off and objectify a sequence of speaking with a single "He said," and the bewildering sense of fall from such an Edenic position, is manifest in Mrs. Quickly's account of what Master Tisick said:

> and, as he said to me—'twas no longer ago than
> Wednesday last, i' good faith—'Neighbor Quickly,'
> says he—Master Dumb our minister was by
> then—'Neighbor Quickly,' says he, 'receive those that
> are civil, for' said he, 'you are
> in an ill name'—now a said so. . . .
>
> (*2H4*, II.iv.83–88)

X

The subject of time would also seem to have been a natural adjunct of Shakespearean metadrama on the basis of its regular accompaniment of the "metapoetic" parts of the sonnets—those places in which the sonnets are most explicitly about themselves. There, with a conception and use of language much like Richard's, the genre itself is a refuge against the ravages of time, and the sonnets thus provide a good "control" for appreciating the special Shakespearean weight of the metadramatic argument in the Lancastrian tetralogy.

What we see, what the subject of time helps us see, is the enactment in the first three plays of a large aesthetic choice which Shakespeare was making at the time: the shift of allegiance to the genre of drama. And we see through the tetralogy an increasingly clear consciousness of deep contradictions between that choice and the rationale of the sonnets. In terms of the sanctions and motives for literature elaborately and authoritatively embodied in the sonnets, allegiance to the genre of drama seems unjustifiable. The choice is already made in *R2* since the genre there is drama; but that play reenacts the choice, which is relished as it "pays off" in *1H4*. Yet building through both these plays is something which dominates *2H4*, something like a bemused wondering about the genre, and about the apparent incomprehensibility of allegiance to a form which, incidentally because it is theatrical and essentially because it consists of a story without a teller, seems sworn brother to cormorant and devouring time.

When we come to the reign of Henry V, however, we find that the distinctive difficulties of the genre are transcended without being denied, so that the "fall" from the language of nondramatic literary forms proves fortunate and the shift of allegiance to drama is sanctioned. This effect is achieved mainly through the character of Hal himself. His career in the tetralogy makes him virtually a figure or embodiment of the genre, waiting through the *H4* plays until he comes into his own in *H5*. It is only after allegiance has shifted away from Richard's nondramatic language that Hal makes his appearance. In the *H4* plays his mood follows the changing status of the genre—playful and spirited in *1H4*, "exceeding weary" in *2H4*. And when, at the end of *H5*, the Chorus moves *from* the idea of the play—

> Thus far, with rough and all-unable pen,
>   Our bending author hath pursu'd the story;
> In little room confining mighty men,
>   Mangling by starts the full course of their glory
>   (Epilogue.1–4)

through a notion of "time" which is at once Hal's life and the play's two hours' traffic *to* the idea of Hal's achievements—

> Small time, but in that small most greatly liv'd
>   This star of England: Fortune made his sword,
> By which, the world's best garden he achiev'd
>   (Epilogue.5–7)

there is an almost explicit identification of Hal with the genre. And the same position is suggested for him by his linguistic theory and practice. It is through the rise and predominance of his language that the genre is sanctioned, in particular, with respect to the problem of time.

In *H5*, by adding a purposive prospect to the justling present of *1H4* and the bewildered retrospect of *2H4*, Hal completes the conceptual system in which the verbal action of drama can have significance. His promises are almost models of that significance: they are significant not in spite of temporal order but through it. If in *2H4* the language of drama seems unsanction-able in terms of the "metapoetics" of the sonnets, Hal's prom-ises are linguistic embodiments of the tactic advised in the procreation sonnets, since they are kept in time, and their beauty is fulfilled and perpetuated in their issue. His dramatic language thus, instead of vainly trying to exclude the sonnets' enemy, and instead of surrendering to him helplessly, makes him an ally.

Hal's turning to good account the language of drama's tem-porality is, of course, part and parcel of his conceiving of lan-guage as a medium or means in which to perform acts. Even in this respect, as we have seen, he goes considerably beyond his father to a comparatively sophisticated and well-articulated "theoric" of verbal action. Putting the theory into practice takes him still farther, so that his voice, alone among the many in the tetralogy, adequately fills the dramatic vacuum created by Hen-ry's silence. Hal's willingness to speak within the constraints of the genre provides the material analogous to marble out of which the eternal shape of dramas can be made: not simply language, as in the sonnets, but verbal acts.

XI

The resolution of the Babel theme in Hal's polyglotism also demonstrates that his linguistic domain is that of aestheti-cally unified drama. As we have seen to some extent already, the metadramatic significance in the tetralogy of the Babel theme depends on the ambiguity in "tongue": the variety of languages within the fiction points to the genre's variety of speakers. What, in observing from within the fiction, we term Hal's poly-glotism, then, seems to exemplify the genre's kind of unity. Though no dramatic tongue can have the comprehensiveness and authority of the authorial voice in nondramatic genres (a fact admitted anew in Hal's awareness of the limitations of his own word), the possibility of translation does admit a common ground on which all of the tongue's meanings may rest.

On the surface Hal's polyglotism concerns structural features of the various languages. At base, though, it seems to have more to do with the nature of the acts performed in those languages: thus his resolution of the Babel theme essentially reflects his resolution of the theme of time. Since dramatic language constitutes verbal action,[15] there are in the world of drama, just as in the real world, standards of judgment and assessment: we judge verbal acts, like nonverbal acts, on the basis of shared moral grounds. In making even the most rudimentary "sense" of the text we use categories which, while language-specific, are deeper and more general than the categories with which we distinguish one tongue from another: in French as in English one can praise, slander, warn, promise, and validly be judged for one's act without reference to the language in which it is performed.

Hal's accession to the throne sanctions drama because his linguistic domain is one in which men can, and must, talk to each other, and in which their speech is morally intelligible. This is signalled by his brothers' meeting "like men that had forgot to speak" (2H4. V.ii.22), by his calling of Parliament and, most notably, by his rejection of Falstaff, in which we can see Shakespeare's refusal to let drama decline into a theatrical Babel, based on a recognition that drama is consistent in its own terms. Falstaff's threat to the genre turns out to be as illusory as that posed by Richard. The existence of other voices makes the extradramatic appeal of Falstaff's voice, like that of Richard's, a kind of time wasting. And what we have seen happen only figuratively to Richard in York's metaphor—the rendering of his language as "tedious prattle" by the genre—actually does happen to Falstaff (if we accept Theobald's emendation) when he dies babbling.

In H5 extradramatic address is localized in the Chorus, who stands outside the drama. Within the drama we have Hal's dramatic speech made monumental in the royal message sequence. And, more generally, we have characters whose interactions comprise a dramatic unity

> Congreeing in a full and natural close,
> Like music.
>
> (H5, I.ii.182–83)

[15]More specifically, a portion of the text has the status of a transcription of the utterance in which the illocutionary act is performed.

XII

The unity like that of "broken music" which Hal's reign establishes is thus relative and communal. Though there is no voice with absolute comprehensive authority, there is nevertheless a standard of judgment in the broken music created by the interactions of the voices. Speaking theologically, this is to say that there is no single divine or divinely sanctioned voice, as Richard takes his to be, but that something like divine authority inheres in the harmony produced by all the voices. Thus when, at the end of *H5*, Queen Isabel asks God to speak, her request is in a sense granted:

> *Q. Isa.* God speak this Amen!
> *All.* Amen.
>
> (*H5*, V.ii.386–87)

The moral-aesthetic unity that is the product of all the voices in a drama is the perfectly absolute and comprehensive verbal standard by which each voice is judged.

This standard, like the harmony of "broken music," is determined by the work but is not locatable within it. Rather, it is to be found in the minds of the work's audience. Whether or not the characters understand each other—whether they glimpse much or little of the basis for judgment comprised by "*All*"—the audience can and must understand them all.

Thus, because drama assumes, depends on, and creates the audience which makes sense of the action by exercising a shared moral intelligence, its unity is in a sense theatrical. But since the audience need not be seated in a theater to perceive the work's unity, this "theatricality" is inherent in the drama. From Richard's theatrical nondramatic language we move through Bolingbroke's untheatrical dramatic "silence" to Hal's realm, in which the verbal action is theatrical *in being* dramatic, that is, in which the characters, instead of appealing to us directly, are found to appeal more or less as they interact with each other.

It would seem, then, that two peculiar features of *H5*, the frequent mention of God and the device of the Chorus, are basically similar with respect to the sanctioning of the genre.

The removal of God from the drama effected by Hal's prayer and by his frequent mention of God seems analogous to the Chorus's separation of the action of the drama from the audience. One might say that the analogy betokens a view of God as an audience of human action. But since here we are concerned not with theology but with metadrama it seems better to say that in *H5*, in the last stage of the metadramatic argument of the tetralogy, the genre of drama is viewed as raising its audience to the position of a God in many persons, judging and assessing in concert the broken music of the action. The implication is that ideally, at least for Shakespeare, the genre would create a universal God consisting of nothing less than *"All"* humanity.

※ A Selective Bibliography

I. *Primary Texts: Shakespeare and Marlowe*

Case, R. H. *The Works and Life of Christopher Marlowe*. New York: Dial Press, 1930–60.

Humphreys, A. R., ed. *William Shakespeare: The First Part of King Henry IV*. Cambridge, Mass.: Harvard University Press, 1960.

——— . *William Shakespeare: The Second Part of King Henry IV*. Cambridge, Mass.: Harvard University Press, 1966.

Sisson, Charles Jasper, ed. *William Shakespeare: The Complete Works*. London: Odhams Press, 1954.

Ure, Peter, ed. *William Shakespeare: King Richard II*. Cambridge, Mass.: Harvard University Press, 1956.

Walter, J. H., ed. *William Shakespeare: King Henry V*. Cambridge, Mass.: Harvard University Press, 1954.

II. *Scholarly and Critical Studies of the Elizabethan Drama*

Abbot, E. A. *A Shakespearian Grammar*. London: Macmillan, 1881.

Adams, John C. *The "Globe" Playhouse*. Cambridge, Mass.: Harvard University Press, 1942.

Altick, Richard D. "Symphonic Imagery in *R2*." *PMLA* 62 (1947): 339–65.

Arnold, Morris LeRoy. *The Soliloquies of Shakespeare*. New York: Columbia University Press, 1911.

Baldwin, T. W. *William Shakespeare's Small Latin and Less Greek*. Urbana: University of Illinois Press, 1944.

Barber, C. L. *Shakespeare's Festive Comedy*. Princeton: Princeton University Press, 1959.

Barton, Anne. "Shakespeare and the Limits of Language." *Shakespeare Survey* 24 (1971): 19–30.

Battenhouse, Roy W. "The Significance of Hamlet's Advice to the Players." In *The Drama of the Renaissance: Essays for Leicester Bradner*, edited by Elmer M. Blistein. Providence: Brown University Press, 1970.

Beckerman, Bernard. *Shakespeare at the Globe*. New York: Macmillan, 1962.

Bentley, Gerald Eades. *The Jacobean and Caroline Stage*. Oxford: Oxford University Press, 1941–56.

———. *Shakespeare and his Theatre*. Lincoln: University of Nebraska Press, 1964.

———. "Shakespeare and the Blackfriars Theatre," *Shakespeare Survey* 1 (1948): 38–50.

Berman, Ronald. *A Reader's Guide to Shakespeare's Plays: A Discursive Bibliography*. Chicago: University of Chicago Press, 1965.

———. "Shakespeare's Alexander: Henry V." *College English* 23 (1962): 532–39.

Berry, Francis. *The Shakespeare Inset*. London: Routledge and Kegan Paul, 1965.

Bethell, Samuel Leslie. "The Comic Element in Shakespeare's Histories." *Anglia* 71 (1952): 82–101.

———. *Shakespeare and the Popular Dramatic Tradition*. London: Staples Press, 1944.

———. "Shakespeare's Actors." *Review of English Studies*, n.s. 1 (1950): 193–205.

Bevington, David M. *From Mankind to Marlowe: Growth of Structure in the Popular Dramatic Tradition*. London, 1944. Cambridge, Mass.: Harvard University Press, 1962.

Bogard, Travis. "Shakespeare's Second Richard." *PMLA* 70 (1955): 205–26.

Bonnard, Georges A. "The Actor in Richard II." *Shakespeare-Jahrbuch* 87 (1952): 87–101.

Bradbrook, Muriel Clara. "Fifty Years of the Criticism of Shakespeare's Style: A Retrospect." *Shakespeare Survey* 7 (1954): 1–12.

———. *The Growth and Structure of Elizabethan Comedy*. London: Chatto and Windus, 1955.

Brown, John Russell. *Shakespeare's Plays in Performance*. London: Edward Arnold, 1966.

Bullough, Geoffrey, ed. *Narrative and Dramatic Sources of Shakespeare.* New York, Columbia University Press, 1957–75.

Burckhardt, Sigurd. *Shakespearean Meanings.* Princeton: Princeton University Press, 1968.

Burton, Dolores M. *Shakespeare's Grammatical Style: A Computer-Assisted Analysis of "Richard II" and "Antony and Cleopatra."* Austin: University of Texas Press, 1973.

Burns, L. "Three Views of *Henry V.*" *Drama Survey* I (1962): 278–300.

Cain, H. E. "Further Light on the Relations of *1* and *2 Henry IV.*" *Shakespeare Quarterly* 2 (1952): 21–38.

Calderwood, James L. *Shakespearean Metadrama.* Minneapolis: University of Minnesota Press, 1971.

―――. "*1 Henry IV*: Art's Gilded Lie." *English Literary Renaissance* 3 (1973): 131–44.

Campbell, Lily Bess. *Shakespeare's 'Histories': Mirrors of Elizabethan Policy.* San Marino, Calif.: Huntington Library, 1947.

Chambers, Sir Edmund Kerchever. *The Elizabethan Stage.* Oxford: Clarendon Press, 1923.

―――. *Shakespeare: A Survey.* London: Sidgwick and Jackson, 1925.

―――. *William Shakespeare: A Study of Facts and Problems.* Oxford: Clarendon Press, 1930.

Charlton, Henry Buckley. *Shakespeare: Politics and Politicians.* Oxford: Oxford University Press, 1929.

Clemen, Wolfgang. *The Development of Shakespeare's Imagery.* London: Methuen, 1951.

―――. *Shakespeare's Soliloquies.* Oxford: Cambridge University Press, 1964.

Craig, Hardin. "Shakespeare and Formal Logic." *Studies in English Philology: A Miscellany in Honor of Frederick Klaeber,* edited by Kemp Malone and Martin B. Ruud. Minneapolis: University of Minnesota Press, 1929.

―――. "Shakespeare and the History Play." *Joseph Quincy Adams Memorial Studies,* edited by James F. McManaway, Giles E. Dawson, and Edwin E. Willoughby. Washington, D. C., 1948.

Crane, Milton. *Shakespeare's Prose.* Chicago: University of Chicago Press, 1951.

Danson, Lawrence. *Tragic Alphabet: Shakespeare's Drama of Language,* New Haven: Yale University Press, 1974.

David, Richard. "Shakespeare in the Waterloo Road." *Shakespeare Survey* 5 (1952): 125–39.

———. "Shakespeare's History Plays: Epic or Drama?" *Shakespeare Survey* 6 (1953): 129–39.

DeBanke, Cécile. *Shakespearean Stage Production: Then and Now.* London: Hutchinson, 1954.

Dean, Leonard F. "Richard II: the State and the Image of the Theater." *PMLA* 67 (1952): 211–18.

———. "*Richard II* to *Henry V*: A Closer View." In *Studies in Honor of De Witt T. Starnes*, edited by Thomas P. Harrison and others. Austin: University of Texas Press, 1967.

Dorius, Raymond Joel. *Discussions of Shakespeare's Histories.* Boston: Heath, 1964.

Draper, John W. "The Character of Richard II." *Philological Quarterly* 21 (1942): 228–36.

———. "The Honor of Corporal Nym." *Shakespeare Association Bulletin* 13 (1938): 131–38.

Ellis-Fermor, Una. *The Frontiers of the Drama.* London: Methuen, 1945.

Empson, William. "Falstaff and Mr. Dover Wilson." *Kenyon Review* 15, no. 2 (Spring 1953): 213–62.

———. *Seven Types of Ambiguity.* New York: Harcourt, 1931.

———. *Some Versions of Pastoral.* London: Chatto and Windus, 1935.

———. *The Structure of Complex Words.* New York: New Directions, 1951.

Evans, Benjamin Ifor. *The Language of Shakespeare's Plays.* London: Methuen, 1952.

Faber, M. D. "Falstaff Behind the Arras." *American Imago* 27, no. 3 (1970): 197–225.

Fergusson, Francis. *The Idea of a Theater.* Princeton: Princeton University Press, 1949.

Flatter, Richard. *Hamlet's Father.* New Haven: Yale University Press, 1949.

Gerstner-Hirzel, Arthur. *The Economy of Action and Word in Shakespeare's Plays.* Berne: Franke Verlag, 1957.

Gilbert, Allan. "Patriotism and Satire in *Henry V*," *Studies in Shakespeare,* edited by Arthur D. Matthews and Clark M. Emery. Coral Gables, Fla.: University of Miami Press, 1953.

Gottschalk, Paul A. "Hal and the 'Play Extempore' in *I Henry IV*." *Texas Studies in Literature and Language* 15 (1974): 604–14.

Granville-Barker, Harley. *Prefaces to Shakespeare.* London, 1927–48.

————. "Shakespeare's Dramatic Art." In *A Companion to Shakespeare Studies,* edited by Harley Granville-Barker and G. B. Harrison. Cambridge: Cambridge University Press, 1934.

Greg, Walter Wilson. *Dramatic Documents from the Elizabethan Playhouses: Stage Plots, Actors' Parts, Prompt Books.* Oxford: Clarendon Press, 1964.

Grivelet, Michel. "Shakespeare's War with Time: The Sonnets and *Richard II." Shakespeare Survey* 23 (1970): 69–78.

Harbage, Alfred. *Shakespeare and the Rival Traditions.* New York: Macmillan, 1952.

————. *Shakespeare's Audience.* New York: Columbia University Press, 1941.

————. *Theatre for Shakespeare.* Toronto: University of Toronto Press, 1955.

Harrison, George Bagshawe. *Elizabethan Plays and Players.* Ann Arbor: University of Michigan Press, 1956.

Hemmingway, S. B. "On Behalf of That Falstaff." *Shakespeare Quarterly* 2 (1952): 307–11.

Hibbard, G. R. "Words, Action, and Artistic Economy." *Shakespeare Survey* 23 (1970): 49–58.

Hollindale, Peter. *A Critical Commentary on Shakespeare's "King Henry IV Part 2."* London: Macmillan, 1971.

Hotson, Leslie. *Shakespeare's Sonnets Dated.* New York: Oxford University Press, 1949.

Hulme, Hilda Mary. *Explorations in Shakespeare's Language.* London: Longmans, 1962.

Hunter, G. K. "Shakespeare's Politics and the Rejection of Falstaff." *Critical Quarterly* 1 (1955): 299–36.

————. "Henry IV and the Elizabethan Two-Part Play." *Review of English Studies,* n.s. 5 (1954): 235–48.

Jenkins, Harold. "Shakespeare's History Plays: 1900–1951," *Shakespeare Survey* 6 (1953): 1–15.

————. *The Structural Problem in Shakespeare's Henry the Fourth.* London: Methuen, 1956.

Jorgensen, Paul. "Accidental Judgements, Casual Slaughters and Purposes Mistook: Critical Reactions to Shakespeare's *Henry V." Shakespeare Association Bulletin* 22 (1947), 51–61.

————. *Redeeming Shakespeare's Words.* Berkeley: University of California Press, 1962.

Kantorowicz, Ernst H. *The King's Two Bodies*. Princeton: Princeton University Press, 1957.

Keeton, George Williams. *Shakespeare's Legal and Political Background*. London: Pitman, 1967.

Knight, George Wilson. *The Wheel of Fire*. London: Oxford University Press, 1930.

———. *The Imperial Theme*. London: Oxford University Press, 1931.

———. *The Olive and the Sword*. London, Oxford University Press, 1944.

———. *Principles of Shakespearian Production*. London: Faber and Faber, 1936.

———. *The Sovereign Flower*. London: Methuen, 1958.

Knights, Lionel Charles. *Drama and Society in the Age of Jonson*. London: Chatto and Windus, 1937.

———. *Some Shakespearean Themes*. London: Chatto and Windus, 1959.

Knowles, Richard. "Unquiet and the Double Plot of 2H4." *Shakespeare Studies* 2 (1966): 133–40.

Kris, E. "Prince Hal's Conflict." *Psychoanalytic Quarterly* 17 (1948): 487–506.

La Guardia, Eric. "Ceremony and History: The Problem of Symbol from *Richard II* to *Henry V*." *Pacific Coast Studies in Shakespeare*, edited by W. F. McNeir and T. N. Greenfield. Eugene: Oregon University Press, 1966.

Law, R. A. "Links Between Shakespeare's History Plays." *Studies in Philology* 24 (1927): 223–42.

Langbaum, Robert Woodrow. *The Poetry of Experience*. London: Chatto and Windus, 1957.

Leech, Clifford. *Shakespeare: The Chronicles*. London: Longmans, Green, 1962.

———. "The Two-Part Play: Marlowe and the Early Shakespeare." *Shakespeare-Jahrbuch* 94 (1958): 90–106.

———. "The Unity of 2 *Henry IV*," *Shakespeare Survey* 6 (1953): 16–24.

McLuhan, Herbert M. "Henry IV: A Mirror for Magistrates." *University of Toronto Quarterly* 17 (1947): 152–60.

McPeek, James A. S. "Richard and His Shadow World," *American Imago* 15 (1958): 195–212.

Mack, Maynard. "The World of Hamlet." *Yale Review* 41 (1952): 502–23.

————. *King Lear in Our Time.* Berkeley: University of California Press, 1965.

Mack, Maynard, Jr. *Killing the King: Three Studies in Shakespeare's Tragic Structure.* New Haven: Yale University Press, 1973.

Mahood, Molly Maureen. *Shakespeare's Wordplay.* London: Methuen, 1957.

Manheim, Michael. *The Weak King Dilemma in the Shakespearean History Play.* Syracuse: Syracuse University Press, 1973.

Mathews, Honor. *Character and Symbol in Shakespeare's Plays.* Cambridge: Cambridge University Press, 1962.

Maveety, Stanley R. "A Second Fall of Cursed Man: The Bold Metaphor in *Richard II.*" *Journal of English and Germanic Philology* 72 (1973): 175–93.

Maxwell, J. C. "Simple or Complex?" *Durham University Journal* 46 (1954): 112–15.

Merchant, W. M. "The Status and Person of Majesty." *Shakespeare-Jahrbuch.* 90 (1954): 285–89.

Messiaen, Pierre. "Drames historiques de Shakespeare: style oratoire, style lyrique, style dramatique." *Revue universitaire* 47 (1939): 23–31.

Morgann, Maurice. *An Essay on the Dramatic Character of Sir John Falstaff* (1777). Edited by W. A. Gill. London: W. Frowde, 1912.

Nicoll, Allardyce and Josephine, eds. *Holinshed's Chronicles as Used in Shakespeare's Plays.* London: J. M. Dent, 1927.

Odell, George Clinton Densmore. *Shakespeare: From Betterton to Irving.* New York: Scribner's, 1920.

Ornstein, Robert. *A Kingdom for a Stage: The Achievement of Shakespeare's History Plays.* Cambridge, Mass.: Harvard University Press, 1972.

Palmer, John Leslie. *Political Characters of Shakespeare.* London: Macmillan, 1945.

Peacock, Ronald. *The Art of Drama.* London: Routledge and Kegan Paul, 1957.

Pierce, Robert B. *Shakespeare's History Plays: The Family and the State.* Columbus: Ohio State University Press, 1971.

Ploch, Georg. "Über den Dialog in den Dramen Shakespeares und seiner Vorläufer." *Geissener Beiträge zur Erforschung der Sprache und Kultur Englands und Nordamerikas,* 2, no. 2 (1925): 129–92.

Prior, Moody E. *The Drama of Power: Studies in Shakespeare's History Plays.* Evanston, Ill.: Northwestern University Press, 1973.

Quinn, Michael. "The King is Not Himself." *Studies in Philology* 56 (1959): 169–86.

Reese, M. M. *The Cease of Majesty: A Study of Shakespeare's History Plays.* London, 1961.

Ribner, Irving. "Bolingbroke, A True Machiavellian," *Modern Language Quarterly* 9 (1948): 177–84.

———. *The English History Play in the Age of Shakespeare.* Princeton: Princeton University Press, 1957.

———. "The Political Problem in Shakespeare's Lancastrian Tetralogy." *Studies in Philology* 49 (1952): 171–84.

Richmond, Hugh M. *Shakespeare's Political Plays.* New York: Random House, 1962.

Righter, Anne. *Shakespeare and the Idea of the Play.* London: Chatto and Windus, 1967.

Rossiter, A. P. "Ambivalence: The Dialectic of the Histories." In *Angel With Horns.* New York: Longmans, 1969.

Sanders, Wilbur. *The Dramatist and the Received Idea.* London: Cambridge University Press, 1968.

Schuchter, J. D. "Prince Hal and Francis: The Imitation of an Action." *Shakespeare Studies* 3 (1967): 129–37.

Sewell Arthur. *Character and Society in Shakespeare.* Oxford: Clarendon Press, 1951.

Shaaber, M. A., "The Unity of *Henry IV.*" *Joseph Quincy Adams Memorial Studies,* edited by James G. McManaway, Giles E. Dawson, and Edwin E. Willoughby. Washington, D.C.: Folger Shakespeare Library, 1948.

Sisson, Charles Jasper. *New Readings in Shakespeare.* Cambridge: Cambridge University Press, 1956.

Small, S. A. "The Reflective Element in Falstaff." *Shakespeare Association Bulletin* 14 (1939): 108–21, 131–43.

Spencer, Theodore. *Shakespeare and the Nature of Man.* New York: Macmillan, 1942.

Sprague, Arthur Colby. "Gadshill Revisited." *Shakespeare Quarterly* 4 (1953): 125–37.

———. *Shakespeare and the Audience: A Study in the Technique of Exposition.* Cambridge, Mass.: Harvard University Press, 1935.

———. *Shakespearian Players and Performances.* Cambridge, Mass.: Harvard University Press, 1953.

Sternlicht, Sanford. "The Making of a Political Martyr-Myth: Shakespeare's Use of the Memory of Richard II in *1 & 2 Henry IV* and *Henry V.*" *Ball State University Forum* 12 (1971): 28–38.

Stewart, John Innes Mackintosh. *Character and Motive in Shakespeare*. London: Longmans, 1949.

Stirling, Thomas Brents. "Bolingbroke's 'Decision'." *Shakespeare Quarterly* 2 (1951) 27–34.

Stoll, Elmer Edgar. *Art and Artifice in Shakespeare's Plays*. Cambridge: Cambridge University Press, 1934.

———. *Poets and Playwrights*. Minneapolis: University of Minnesota Press, 1930.

———. *Shakespeare Studies*. New York: Macmillan, 1927.

Styan, John Louis. *The Elements of Drama*. Cambridge: Cambridge University Press, 1960.

———. *Shakespeare's Stagecraft*. Cambridge: Cambridge University Press, 1967.

Tillyard, E. M. W. "Shakespeare's Historical Cycle: Organism or Compilation." *Studies in Philology* 51 (1954): 34–39, (rejoinder by R. A. Law, *ibid.*, pp. 40–41).

———. *Shakespeare's History Plays*. London: Chatto and Windus, 1944.

Traversi, Derek A. *Shakespeare from "Richard II" to "Henry IV."* Stanford, Calif.: Stanford University Press, 1957.

Trewin, John Courtenay. *Shakespeare on the English Stage, 1900–1964*. London: Barrie and Rockliff, 1964.

Van Laan, Thomas F. *The Idiom of Drama*. Ithaca, N.Y.: Cornell University Press, 1970.

Wales, Julia G. *Character and Action in Shakespeare*. Madison: University of Wisconsin Press, 1923.

Watkins, Ronald. *On Producing Shakespeare*. 2d ed. New York: Benjamin Blom, 1964.

Webber, Joan. "The Renewal of the King's Symbolic Role: From *Richard II* to *Henry V.*" *Texas Studies in Literature and Language* 4 (1963): 530–38.

Willcock, G. D. "Shakespeare and Elizabethan English." *Shakespeare Survey* 7 (1954): 12.

Wilson, Frank Percy. *Marlowe and Early Shakespeare*. Oxford: Clarendon Press, 1955.

Wilson, J. Dover. *The Fortunes of Falstaff*. New York: Macmillan, 1944.

———. "The Political Background of Shakespeare's *Richard II* and *Henry IV.*" *Shakespeare-Jahrbuch* 75 (1939): 36–51.

Wilson, J. Dover, and Worsley, T. C. *Shakespeare's Histories at Stratford, 1951*. London: M. Reinhardt, 1952.

Winny, James. *The Player King: A Theme of Shakespeare's Histories*. New York: Barnes and Noble, 1968.

III. *Speech Action: Philosophical, Linguistic and Critical Theory*

Austin, John Langshawe. *How to Do Things with Words.* Edited by J. O. Urmson. Oxford: Clarendon Press, 1962.

————. *Philosophical Papers.* Edited by J. O. Urmson and G. J. Warnock. Oxford: Clarendon Press, 1961.

————. *Sense and Sensibilia.* Edited by G. J. Warnock. Oxford: Clarendon Press, 1962.

Berlin, Isaiah, et al. *Essays on J. L. Austin.* Oxford: Clarendon Press, 1973.

Boyd, Julian, and Thorne, J. P. "The Deep Grammar of Model Verbs," *ERIC/PEGS* (Center for Applied Linguistics, Washington, D.C.) 31 (16 April 1968).

Campbell, B. G. "Toward a Workable Taxonomy of Illocutionary Forces, and its Implication for Works of Imaginative Literature." *Language and Style* 8, no. 1 (Winter 1975): 3–20.

Eaton, Marcia. "Speech Acts: A Bibliography." *Centrum* 2, no. 2 (1974): 57–72.

Fish, Stanley E. "How to Do Things with Austin and Searle: Speech Act Theory and Literary Criticism." *Modern Language Notes* 91, no. 5 (1976): 983–1025.

Grice, H. P. "Logic and Conversation," In *Speech Acts.* Syntax and Semantics, vol. 3, edited by Peter Cole and Jerry L. Morgan. New York: Seminar Press, 1975.

Jespersen, Otto. *Language: Its Nature, Development and Origin.* London: George Allen and Unwin, 1922.

————. *The Philosophy of Grammar.* London: George Allen and Unwin, 1924.

Ohmann, Richard. "Instrumental Style: Notes on the Theory of Speech as Action." In *Current Trends in Stylistics.* Papers in Linguistics Monograph Series, vol. 2, edited by Braj B. Kachru, pp. 115–41. Edmonton and Champaign, Ill.: Linguistic Research, 1972.

————. "Literature as Act." In *Approaches to Poetics,* edited by Seymour Chatman, pp. 83–97. New York: Columbia University Press, 1973.

Pratt, Mary Louise. *Toward a Speech Act Theory of Literary Discourse.* Bloomington: University of Indiana Press, 1977.

Rorty, Richard, ed. *The Linguistic Turn: Recent Essays in Philosophical Method.* Chicago: University of Chicago Press, 1967.

Searle, John R. *Speech Acts: An Essay in the Philosophy of Language.* Cambridge: Cambridge University Press, 1969.

————. "Indirect Speech Acts." In *Speech Acts. Syntax and Semantics*, vol. 3, ed. Peter Cole and Jerry L. Morgan, pp. 59–82. New York: Seminar Press, 1975.

————. "The Logical Status of Fictional Discourse." *New Literary History* 6, no. 2 (1975): 319–32.

————. "A Taxonomy of Illocutionary Acts." In *Language, Mind, and Knowledge*. Minnesota Studies in the Philosophy of Science, vol. 7, edited by Keith Gunderson, pp. 344–69. Minneapolis: University of Minnesota Press, 1975.

Shiffer, Stephen R. *Meaning*. Oxford: Clarendon Press, 1972.

Turner, Roy, ed. *Ethnomethodology: Selected Readings*. Harmondsworth, Eng.: Penguin, 1974.

Wallace, Karl Richards. *Understanding Discourse: The Speech Act and Rhetorical Action*. Baton Rouge: Louisiana State University Press, 1973.

Whorf, B. L. *Language, Thought and Reality*. Edited by John B. Carroll. Cambridge, Mass.: Technology Press of M.I.T., 1956.

IV. *Other Works*

Duncan, Starkey, Jr. "Some Signals and Rules for Taking Speaking Turns in Conversations." *Journal of Personality and Social Psychology* 23 (1972): 283–92; reprinted in *Nonverbal Communication*, edited by Shirley Weitz, pp. 298–311. New York: Oxford University Press, 1974.

Scholes, Robert, and Kellogg, Robert. *The Nature of Narrative*. New York: Oxford University Press, 1966.

Steiner, George. *After Babel: Aspects of Language and Translation*. London: Oxford University Press, 1974.

Tilley, Morris Palmer. *A Dictionary of the Proverbs in England in the Sixteenth and Seventeenth Centuries*. Ann Arbor: University of Michigan Press, 1950.

Von Rand, Gerhard. *Genesis: A Commentary*. Translated by John H. Marks. Philadelphia: Westminster Press, 1961.

Wright, George T. "The Lyric Present: Simple Present Verbs in English Poems." *PMLA* 89 (1974): 563–79.

❀ Index

Designer: Al Burkhardt
Compositor: Viking Typographics
Printer: Thomson-Shore, Inc.
Binder: Thomson-Shore, Inc.
Text: VIP Palatino
Display: VIP Palatino
Cloth: Holliston Roxite A Linen Finish 50363
Paper: 50 lb Bookmark